2.

Barcelona

Insight Compact Guide: Barcelona is the ultimate quick-reference guide to the Catalan capital. It tells you all you need to know about Barcelona's attractions, from its peaceful parks to the bustling Ramblas, the sparkling modern port to the ancient Gothic Quarter and stunning avant-garde architecture to priceless museum collections.

This is one of over 100 titles in Insight Guides' series of pocket-sized, easy-to-use guidebooks intended for the independent-minded traveller. Compact Guides are in essence travel encyclopedias in miniature, designed to be comprehensive yet portable, as well as up-to-date and authoritative.

D0933328

Star Attractions

An instant reference
to some of
Barcelona's most
popular tourist
attractions to help
you on your way.

The Ramblas p17

La Boqueria p19

Plaça Reial p22

Catedral La Seu p30

Museu Picasso p37

Museu d'Art de
Catalunya p42

Casa Batlló p48

Sagrada Família p51

Parc Güell p59

Tibidabo p60

Sitges p70

Barcelona

Introduction

Barcelona – A Feast for the Eyes 5
Historical Highlights 10

Places

Route 1: Around the Ramblas 16
Route 2: Barri Gòtic 25
Route 3: The Port and La Ribera..32
Route 4: Montjuïc..40
Route 5: Passeig de Gràcia – Templo de la
Sagrada Família 46
Route 6: Pedralbes and the surrounding area 53

Additional Sights...56
Excursions:
       Tibidabo – Sant Cugat del Vallès................................60
       Montserrat – Terrassa..64
       Sitges – Vilafranca – Martorell 69

Culture

Art History 75
Festivals and Folklore..80

Leisure

Food and Drink 83
Shopping and Markets 87
Nightlife 89

Practical Information

Getting There 93
Getting Around 95
Facts for the Visitor...97
Accommodation...102

Index 104

Barcelona – A Feast for the Eyes

Opposite: La Sagrada Família

When locals and tourists jostle together on the viewing platform of the Columbus Monument to get a view over the harbour and the old city – with Mount Tibidabo as the backdrop to the west – one phrase is heard over and over again: *'qué magnífico'* – 'what a wonderful city'. Barcelona is certainly a feast for the eyes, and the first view of this metropolis from the air – whether from the Columbus Monument, from the Olympic mountain of Montjuïc or from Tibidabo – impresses every visitor with its beauty and dimensions.

Like the rings of a tree, new areas are forever growing up around the original core, the Gothic Quarter in the heart of the historical old city. To the west, the regular chessboard-like pattern of the streets in the Eixample district is particularly striking, overlooked by the unconventional towers of Antoni Gaudí's Sagrada Família cathedral. To the south, Montjuïc was spruced up for the Olympic Games in 1992. To the north, between the Olympic village and the marina, are the two tower blocks in the Parc de Mar, symbols of the modern development of the city as well as Barcelona's new gateway to the sea.

Visitors soon find themselves caught up in the turmoil of day to day life in this hectic capital city. The sun barely penetrates the narrow side streets of the old town, even in summer. The crumbling plaster of the facades reflects the poverty of many districts. On the boulevards you'll be surrounded by traffic – sometimes thundering along, at other times stationary – as you visit the open-air museum which is Barcelona. The city compensates visitors for their stress, however, with numerous culinary oases and musical delights, whether classical or disco. Everything in Barcelona has its positive and negative sides.

Catalonia's capital

Barcelona is the capital of the autonomous region of Catalonia. Although part of Spain's constitutional monarchy, since 1979 *Catalunya* has had its own independent government and administration, the *Generalitat.* For long periods Catalonia developed independently of the other areas of the Iberian peninsula. In the 13th and 14th centuries, Catalonia became the leading power in the Mediterranean area. Later, numerous attempts were made to break away from the Spanish empire, but these independence movements were always put down. The worst period, however, was under Franco, when virtually any expression of national independence was forbidden, including the Catalan language. Even today, the people of Catalonia are hypersensitive to comments from Madrid about the region's administration, education system or culture.

Statue of Columbus

5

The Catalans have cultivated their own language for over 1000 years. *Català* isn't just another dialect of Spanish, but instead is related to Provençal and Italian. Nowadays *castellano* (Spanish) and *Català* have equal official status, but it is *Català* that people choose to speak. The Catalans are also attempting to revive their own folkloric culture, as can be seen by the numerous festivals both in the city and the surrounding countryside (*see pages 80–81*). The Catalans make no bones about the fact that they see themselves as mid-Europeans rather than Spaniards. '*Europa no comença als Pirineus*' – 'Europe doesn't begin at the Pyrenees' – is one of the latest slogans for an independent Catalonia.

Location and Size

Barcelona, with a population of 1.8 million, is growing so rapidly that it barely has enough room to breathe in the space nature has allotted it. Squeezed between the Montjuïc hill (213m/700 ft) to the south, the foothills of the Serra de Collserola ending with Tibidabo (532m/1745ft) to the west, and the Mediterranean to the southeast, the metropolis is extending its tentacles ever further. On the other side of the hills huge dormitory towns have been created. Some 3 million people are crowded into the greater metropolitan Barcelona area – almost half the total population of Catalonia.

The most densely populated area is the old city centre with almost 2,000 inhabitants per square kilometre (770 per square mile). The proportion of non-Catalan Spaniards and foreigners is high, particularly in the area around the Ramblas. To the north of the Via Laietana, in the Ribera and Barceloneta districts the inhabitants are mainly original Barcelonans. The central Eixample area is more thinly populated, whereas the 'left' and 'right' Eixample are bustling residential districts. The modern apartments and houses in the top residential areas in the west of the city – Pedralbes, Sarrià or Vallvidrera – are considered especially desirable. But the Nova Icària area around the Olympic village – directly by the sea in the north of the city – is also turning into an exclusive area in view of the horrendous property prices. And this is despite the fact that the plans included the building of a number of council flats. Typical worker and dormitory towns can be found on the northern and southern edges of Barcelona, some of which (L'Hospitalet or San Adrià de Besos, for example) have already become major towns in their own right.

'*Barcelona, posa't guapa*' – 'Barcelona, make yourself beautiful' was the motto given by the city's administrators to the desperately needed renovation programme in the city centre. The programme was given a boost by the choice of Barcelona to host the Olympic Games in 199

Twin towers at the Olympic village

Numerous dilapidated houses still collapse each year, while speculators look for properties which can be pulled down and renovated. The archetypal slums of cardboard and tin huts, which used to be found in the outlying areas, are no longer to be seen. Instead there is a depressing mass of concrete council flats. In common with many other large European cities, the original inhabitants of the luxuriously renovated flats in the city centre can no longer afford to pay the rents. Between 1989 and 1991 alone, rents increased by around 30 percent in some parts of the city. Those in the lower income groups are naturally worst hit. Many residents from the old city areas have turned to self-help groups to fight the problem. The so-called *Associacions de veïnatge* (neighbourhood groups) deal not only with tenants' housing problems but also other social issues such as the care of the elderly and children.

What is missing in Barcelona are really large green expanses. Apart from the Parc de la Ciutadella, there is hardly a park in the inner city. The Barcelonans themselves are to blame here. Cerdà's plan for the Eixample area (*see page 75*) included extensive parks and gardens. However, property speculators – and, above all, owners of the almighty motor car – killed off his forward-looking concept. One glimmer of hope comes from the new park areas which were built as part of the concept of *Nou Urbanisme*. It is hoped that these open spaces and recreational areas and the integration of art into Barcelona's daily life will give a new quality to life in the city.

Parc de la Ciutadella

7

One of the positive features of this city is its location on the Mediterranean. Spurred on by Olympic changes, Barcelona has now opened up to the sea and boasts a 5 km (3 mile) waterfront. Apart from the industrial port and the Port Vell, with its marina and Maremagnum commercial centre, there are several kilometres of sandy beaches: from San Sebastià through the Olympic village and ending in an enormous development in Selva de Mar. These are city beaches so cleanliness is dubious, but they have their attractions on sticky summer days and for winter walks.

Rivalries

Anyone who travels to Barcelona or the Costa Brava must know that Barcelona and Madrid, like Catalonia and Andalusia, have virtually nothing in common. The newspapers and magazines are permanently stirring up the latest, albeit peaceful, forms of rivalry between the nation's capital, Madrid, and its economic centre, Barcelona. At stake is which city has the best football team, which the most elegant fashion or the most lively pubs, and which is the top tourist attraction. The causes of this apparently harmless rivalry go back as far as the 16th century. The Span-

Barça football team flags

ish kings in Madrid excluded Barcelona from the sea-trade with the new colonies in America, thus precipitating the economic demise of the city. To this day, the Catalan capital feels that the arrogant administrators in Madrid pay little attention to Barcelona when it comes to distributing public money or awarding large projects.

The relationship between the Catalans and Andalusians is also not exactly unproblematic. This goes back to the dictator Franco, who allowed many workers, particularly from Spain's poorer south, to resettle in Catalonia as a way of weakening Catalan national unity. This explains the terms of abuse which are still sometimes used today. The Catalans call the Andalusians *Loleilos*, because of their Flamenco music, in which the onomatopoeic word 'loleilo' is common. The Andalusians, in turn, call the Catalans *Polacos* (Poles) on account of their 'incomprehensible' language and proverbial obsession with business and a work ethic which dominates their life, leaving no time for dance or music.

Flamenco, music from the south

8

The reality is that most Andalusians and other outsiders have worse employment opportunities than Catalans. And without a knowledge of *Català* it is almost impossible to find a job in the city.

Commerce and Trade

In the past agriculture was the mainstay of the Catalan economy. Nowadays only 6 percent of the population work in the primary sector, with 44 percent in industry and 50 percent in the service sector. Almost half of the 6 million Catalans live and work in the Barcelona area, home of 25 percent of Spain's industrial production. Firms from the metal, chemical and textile branches in particular have set up in the city, whilst the SEAT car works is developing into one of Barcelona's most important employers.

Parc de l'Espanya Industrial

The country's most European Spaniards, as the Catalans like to describe themselves, see their ambitious nature challenged by, among other things, Spain's entrance to the European Union – so much so that they are prepared to change even their most traditional customs. Just adapting their working hours to fit in with mid-European norms represents a major change. Workers at multinational companies often based out of town have had lunch breaks cut to between 30 minutes and an hour. Gone is the extended *siesta* which allowed time for a leisurely meal and relaxation. However, most businesses still respect a 2-hour lunch break but will then remain open until 8 or 9pm. There doesn't even seem to be time anymore for the evening chatter at the bar, enjoying a *tapas* snack to stave off hunger until the evening meal at 10pm. Life in Spain's largest commercial and trade centre is undergoing radical change.

City of Culture

Barcelona is more than just an economic centre. It is also
a cultural metropolis of the first order, which has invested
considerable money in developing its extraordinary po-
tential. Virtually every style of architecture can be found,
with works of art from every epoch. Both in its museums and in the open air, Barcelona reflects the long tradition of art in the city, a tradition which began with the
Romans. Their traces can be found in the Gothic Quarter around the cathedral, where, in the Middle Ages, the
royals and nobility immortalised themselves with splendid buildings. The Museu d'Art de Catalunya (MNAC)
on Montjuïc uniquely documents the art of the Romanesque
and Gothic periods. Among the city's 50 or so museums
– including a shoe museum (Museu del Calçat Antic, *see
page 25*) and a slot-machine museum (Museu d'Autòmates,
see page 62) – are numerous top rate presentations of modern art. Two examples are the Fundació Joan Miró (*see
page 43*) and the Museu Picasso (*see page 37*). Joan Miró
(1893–1983) was born in Barcelona and never wanted his
works to be shut up in rooms. He designed a massive
cobbled mosaic for the Ramblas, in front of the Liceu metro
station. Pablo Picasso (1881–1973) decorated the Association of Architects near the cathedral with a frieze. Antoni Tàpies (born 1923) has established his own exhibition
hall, the Fundació Antoni Tàpies, in a building designed
by art nouveau architect Lluís Domènech i Montaner (*see
page 78*) and crowned with a modern wire sculpture.
Countless books have been published about Barcelona and
art nouveau, or modernism as it is called here (*see page 75*).

Exhibits at the shoe museum

The Fundació Antoni Tàpies

'Girl Escaping' by Miró

Since the beginning of the 1980s Barcelona has blos-
somed into a citadel of modern design. Young artists have
conquered just about every area of life, designing everything from post-modernist furniture and jewellery to complete pubs. Together with the architects of the *Nou
Urbanisme* (new town planning), they have also designed
new facades and rows of houses. One of their most famous
representatives is Xavier Mariscal, who created the mas-
cot for the 1992 Olympic Games, the dog 'Cobi'. He was
also responsible for the decoration of the Gambrinus
restaurant on the Moll de la Fusta.

Open-air art, musical performances and pantomime are
also established parts of the cultural scene. Ten large theatres and three concert halls offer every kind of theatre,
dance and musical event. There is also a lively, semi-pro-
fessional alternative scene. The borders between art and
entertainment could hardly be more fluid. Countless bars,
variety shows and discotheques are just waiting to be discovered, along with more than 70 cinemas, good jazz clubs
and numerous temples of culinary delight. Various tips can
be found on *pages 89 to 91*.

Historical Highlights

c1000BC Many legends have grown up to explain Barcelona's origins. One even has Hercules as the city's founding father. What is certain, however, is that around 700BC the Iberians settled on the fertile area between the Riu Llobregat in the south and the Riu Besòs in the north.

c600BC For the first time the sails of Greek ships appear off the Catalan coast. Among the Greek settlements is Empòrion on the Costa Brava.

c300BC The Carthaginians penetrate as far as Catalonia. According to one legend, Hamilcar Barca, a rich Carthaginian and father of Hannibal, occupied the city and gave it the name Barcino.

264BC After the First Punic War between the Romans and Carthaginians, there are far-reaching changes in the Roman colonies in the Iberian peninsula. When Hannibal crosses the Ebro in 217BC, Romans troops capture Barcelona. In the peace treaty of 197BC the Carthaginians have to give up their Spanish conquests. Rome founds the *Hispania Citerior* with Tarraco (Tarragona) as its capital.

200BC to AD300 Barcelona flourishes, and a magnificent city centre develops around the forum (today Plaça Sant Jaume) on the small hill called Mons Taber (12m/40ft). Around the time of Christ's birth, under the rule of Emperor Augustus, Barcino is renamed Julia Augusta Favencia Paterna Barcino.

AD476 The Visigoths under King Athaulf enter eastern Spain and name their territory south of the Pyrenees 'Gotalonia'. In 476 they capture the city of Barcelona and make it the capital of their Iberian Empire.

Around 700 The Moors from North Africa invade Spain, and capture Barcelona in 713. In 801, however, they are forced out by the Franks. From this time on the Arabic influence on culture and architecture in the city is considerably less marked than, for example, in Andalusia.

8th–9th century The Franks found the Marca Hispanica (Spanish Marches). Under Wilfred the Hairy (Guifré el Pilós) the areas occupied by the Franks south of the Pyrenees are unified to form one single county. He establishes the House of Barcelona, a dynasty that is to continue in an unbroken line for 500 years.

985 Almansur, Grand Vizier of the Caliph Hisham II, reaches Barcelona and destroys large parts of the city. For a short period it takes on the Arabic name Barcaluna. Help comes from the Franks who free the city again.

988 Borell II declares the county of Barcelona autonomous, leading to the continual extension of its territory. The foundation is thereby laid for the development of a Catalonia independent from France. This year is celebrated as the birthdate of the state.

1137 Berenguer IV, Count of Barcelona, marries Petronilla, heiress to the throne of Aragón. Barcelona becomes capital of the kingdom of Aragón and enjoys a period of great success. The Catalonian-Aragón confederation is able to extend its power over the whole Mediterranean area as far as Naples (1284) and Sardinia (1295). The royal family and the nobility erect a number of splendid buildings in Barcelona (the Gothic Quarter or Barri Gòtic, *see page 25*).

By the 14th century Catalonia has become one of the Mediterranean's most formidable maritime nations and its rule book, the *Consolat de Mar*, governs all sea trade.

1359 The *Corts Catalanes*, a representative body of nobility, citizens and priests which had met at irregular intervals since 1289 is officially appointed. A body is set up to regulate financial and political matters. It is later given the name *Generalitat de Catalunya*. The development of the city is sponsored just as much by merchants and guildsmen as by nobles and counts.

1395 Annual competitions for poets and troubadors, called the Jocs Florals, are initiated. They are based on a similar event in Toulouse, for Catalonia, which extends over the Pyrenees into the Rousillon in France, has close links with its neighbour, Languedoc, and their languages are almost the same.

1469 Ferdinand II of Aragón marries Queen Isabella I of Castile. The unification of these Christian kingdoms leads in 1492 to the fall of Grenada, the last bastion of the Moors. Under the developing absolute monarchy of the Catholic Monarchs – a title bestowed on Isabella and Ferdinand by the Pope – Catalonia and Barcelona become less important. Trade with the new colonies in the Americas goes via the Atlantic ports. Madrid becomes the national centre, whilst Barcelona suffers economic decline.

1639 During the Thirty Years War with France, the Catalans rise up against the centralist rule of Philip IV, and are supported by the French king Louis XIII. The Spanish troops are unable to recapture Barcelona until 1651.

1659 In the Treaty of the Pyrennees, all Catalonia north of the Pyrennees is ceded to France.

1714 Barcelona sides with the Habsburgs in the Spanish War of Succession, causing the Bourbon Philip V to take the city on 11 September. He destroys the whole of the Ribera area, abolishes the Corts Catalanes and has a citadel built. Today 11 September (La Diada) is the national day of celebration in Catalonia.

1808 The inhabitants of the city rise up against the French. Napoleon enters Spain and destroys large parts of Barcelona, especially its churches.

Around 1850 From 1814 onwards the city experiences an economic boom under Ferdinand VII. The industrial revolution has a positive effect and Barcelona becomes Spain's leading centre for technical developments. In 1833 the country's first steam-driven engine is working in the city; in 1848 the first train connection between Barcelona and Mataró is built and in 1873 the first electricity plant is constructed. Around the middle of the century, a decision is taken to raze the citadel to the ground. The old city walls are also taken down and the building of the new city (L'Eixample, *see page 75*) begins in 1860.

1888 Barcelona hosts its first Universal Exposition on the site of the former citadel. Numerous modernist buildings are erected throughout the city (*see page 75*).

1914 A Catalonian provincial government, the *Mancomunitat*, is set up but its efforts to establish independence are instantly suppressed by the military dictatorship of Primo de Rivera (1923-1930).

1929 A second Universal Exposition is held on the grounds of Montjuïc. Numerous buildings, including the current Olympic stadium and the Poble Espanyol (*see page 42*) are built.

1932 In the second Spanish republic Catalonia is granted its first statute of independence. Francesc Macià is president of the *Generalitat de Catalunya*. The statute barely takes effect, however, as the Spanish Civil War starts in 1936.

1939 On 26 January Franco's troops enter Barcelona, which is supporting the republic. The dream of independence has to give way to a shattering reality for the next 38 years. Franco forbids any expression of Catalan lifestyle; its language and customs are strictly suppressed. The statute of autonomy is revoked and the president of the Generalitat, Lluís Companys, is executed in the Montjuïc Castle. Spaniards from other parts of the country (above all Andalusia) are resettled in Barcelona to undermine the Catalan national identity and language. Refugee settlements and enormous, barren dormitory towns arise in the suburbs.

1975 After Franco's death a constitutional monarchy is set up by plebiscite in Spain. Juan Carlos proclaimed king in 1975. Catalan (*Català*) recognised as an official language.

1979 Catalonia receives its second statute of autonomy. At the elections of 1980 Jordi Pujol becomes the first president of the region. Since then the capital, Barcelona, has undergone rapid development, with new-found Catalan self-confidence.

1981 A military putsch in Madrid against the still young Spanish democracy is defeated.

1986 Spain becomes a member of the European Community, with full membership from 1993. On 17 October Barcelona is chosen as host for the 1992 Olympic Games. A massive wave of building activity gets under way, and the city moves into the international limelight.

1992 In the year when the 500th anniversary of Columbus's discovery of America is being celebrated, the XXV Olympic Games are held in Barcelona.

1995 Port Vell development completed. Contemporary Art Museum opens.

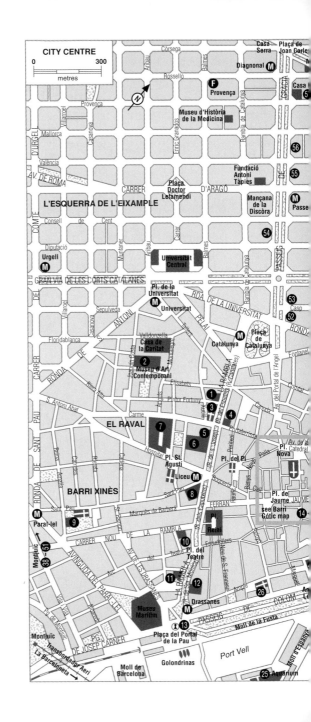

Plaça de Catalunya

Preceding pages: the view from Montjuïc

Route 1

Around the Ramblas

This route along the Ramblas – from the Plaça de Catalunya to the port – also includes many interesting sights in the side streets and nearby squares. Although it is possible to do the walk in half a day, anyone who really wants to discover the fascination of Barcelona's top street will want to allow a full day.

The tour begins at the ★ **Plaça de Catalunya**. This 50,000-sq m (540,000-sq ft) square was laid out following the demolition of the city walls in the middle of the 19th century. It soon developed into a main junction connecting the narrows side streets of the old town with the generously laid out boulevards of the new city. Seven streets join here, and below the surface there is a maze of tunnels and passages, where two train and three metro lines meet. This makes the Plaça de Catalunya an ideal meeting place and the starting point for various excursions all over the city.

Balloon seller

Despite the enormous volume of traffic in the area, it is still possible to enjoy the contemplative atmosphere of the city's green spaces. Young people recline on the lawns around the two fountains which are illuminated at night-time. Locals sit on white metal stools, take time out for a midday break and to read their newspapers. Nobody seems to be bothered by the thousands of pigeons which continually beg for food. Even the agile attendant, who goes round the square wearing his official cap and demanding payment for every chair, is treated with equanimity and receives his money without any questions being asked.

If it wasn't for the non-stop honking of car horns and the faint smell of petrol which sometimes wafts over the popcorn stands, you could imagine that you were on the *Plaça Major* (main square) of a Catalan village. However, you are not on the Costa Brava but in one of Europe's most important economic and trade centres as the surrounding buildings testify. The enormous neo-classical buildings of the large Spanish banks – with neon advertising signs for Japanese businesses on their roofs – bring the dreaming holidaymaker back to reality.

Sculpture in a shopping centre

On the north side of the square is the department store El Corte Inglés. The largest store in the city – a second one from the same chain is on the Avinguda Diagonal – even offers an interpreting service for foreign shoppers. From the roof-terrace of the restaurant on the top floor there is a wonderful, if expensive, view over the old city and towards the sea.

On the corner of Carrer de Pelai is a large new commercial centre, El Triangle, and opposite, two bastions of recent international influence, Marks and Spencer and the Hard Rock Café. And just a few steps away one of the most famous streets in the world, the plane tree-lined **★★★ La Rambla**.

As late as the 13th century this 1.2-km (¾-mile) long pedestrian avenue, which now has cars roaring to the left and right, was still a river bed (*rambla* in Arabic) and formed the southwestern border of the old city. The river wasn't filled in until the 15th century, when the area was integrated into the city and the university was sited here. In the 19th century a promenade was built and plane trees were planted. The Catalans speak of the *Rambles* in the plural (*Ramblas* in Spanish), because it consists of five separate street sections, each of which has its own particular flair. This is Barcelona's most popular street for just strolling along.

17

Canaletes drinking fountains

The first section is the **Rambla de Canaletes**, which is famous for its drinking fountains of the same name. On Saturday these are taken over by the supporters of the FC Barcelona football team. This Rambla, with its lines of white stools, is also a meeting point for political groups and a starting point for demonstrations. Up until 1714, students from the nearby university used to hold their meetings here. (Barcelona then lost its university status for a long time – a punishment by Philip V.) Nowadays you can hear the twittering, cheeping and scratching of the birds and other small animals (apes, turtles, fish, dogs, etc) which are on offer in the little shops. The street is therefore also known as the Rambla dels Ocells (the street of

Busker and birds on the Ramblas

the birds). Further on it becomes the Rambla Sant Josep, with its market of the same name (better known as La Boqueria, *see page 19*). The traditional flower- and plant-sellers have their stalls on this part of the avenue, which has given it its other name, the Rambla de les Flors (the street of the flowers). Next comes the Rambla dels Caputxins, lined with cafés as far as the Plaça Reial. The name of this part of the street comes from the Capuchin monastery which used to be here. The last section, leading down to the waterfront, is the Rambla Santa Mònica, also named after a monastery which used to be here in the Middle Ages.

Another special feature of the Ramblas are the newspaper kiosks which can be found every 100m (330ft) or so. These are popular meeting points, where people come to chat, get the latest newspaper, or buy one of Spain's incredibly popular comics for adults or even a pornographic magazine. Post cards and foreign newspapers are also available.

18

But back to the beginning of the street, to the Rambla de Canaletes. Here, on the right-hand side, jammed between fast food shops, is a restaurant with real tradition. The Nuria has a regular group of local customers who swear by the place on account of its excellent tapas (*see page 83*).

Teatre Poliorama

Further down this side of the street is the **Teatre Poliorama ❶**. Designed by Josep Domènech i Estapà, a contemporary of Gaudí, this theatre specialises in light Catalan productions and has a season for children. On the upper floor is the Science Academy (Acadèmia de Ciències) with a large library.

The Carrer del Pintor Fortuny turns off after the theatre. The street leads to the Carrer dels Àngels, where the 16th-century **Convent dels Àngels** is the designated home of the city's large newspaper library, whose collection includes more than 70,000 titles dating back to 1830. A little further on, in the Carrer Montalegre, is the **Casa de la Caritat**, a former refuge for the poor and homeless of the district and now the CCCB (Centre of Contemporary Culture).

Beside it is the impressive white slab of the new ★★ **Museu d'Art Contemporani – MACBA ❷** (Museum of Contemporary Art; Monday to Friday noon–8pm, Saturday 10am–8pm, Sunday 10am–3pm), a fine space for large abstract work, sculpture and installations. A library, video library and cafeteria have also been incorporated into the complex.

On the way back to the Ramblas (via Carrer d'Elisabets and Carrer d'en Xuclà) it's worth visiting an interesting bar. Los Toreros, in the lower part of Carrer d'en Xuclà (No 3–5), is the regular pub of many bull-fighters and is decorated like a bull-fighting museum. The host himself is a former torero, and will delight in explaining to you his special bull-fighters' drink.

Coming back to the Rambla dels Estudis, there is a church on the corner of Carrer del Carme. This is the **Mare Déu Betlem** church ❸, which was built by Jesuits between 1697 and 1729 and completely burned down during the civil war in 1936. As a result there is little worth seeing inside. The portals are decorated in baroque style. On the other side of the Rambla is the ★ **Palau Mojà** ❹. The facade of this splendid 18th-century palace is still waiting to be renovated. The murals by Catalan painter Francesc Pla in the main salon are particularly interesting. The inner courtyard is also worth visiting, as is the city book shop on the side facing the Rambla. Here you can buy just about every form of literature which has been published about Barcelona and Catalonia.

The walk continues along the Rambla Sant Josep to the ★ **Palau de la Virreina** ❺. This was built between 1772 and 1778 by Marquès de Castellbell, the viceroy of Peru, for his wife. After his death, his widow – the vicereine (*virreina*) – lived here more or less alone. Exhibitions are now shown in the palace. On the ground floor is the city's cultural information centre, and in a side wing there is a treasure trove for music fans: the **Casa Beethoven**, with instruments and scores, both modern and antique.

Exhibition in the Palau Virreina

Casa Beethoven

Near the palace is the entrance to ★★★ **La Boqueria** (literally, the pharynx) ❻, Barcelona's most famous market. Behind the mighty construction of the cast iron portal with its stained glass decorations (from 1835), the appetisingly arranged stands offer everything your heart could desire: fresh vegetables, fresh fish, fruit and so on. On the other hand, the Mercat de Sant Josep, as the market is officially called, has its price. (It is cheaper before 10am, when the Catalans do their shopping.) Prices are lower in the other markets, such as the Mercat Concepció or Santa Caterina. But nowhere else are there such wonderful bars as can be experienced here. The Garduña Bar is particularly well known (*see page 86*).

Fruit stall in La Boqueria

After the market the Carrer de Hospital turns off to the right. This leads first to Plaça Sant Agustí, dominated by the 18th-century Santa Agustí church with its three aisles. A little further on is the Teatre Romea in the tiny Canonge de Colom square. Now over 125 years old, the theatre is home to the city's drama centre, and seems to cower in the shadows of the massive walls of the ★ **Antic Hospital de la Santa Creu** ❼. This building was erected in the 11th century as a refuge for pilgrims. From the 15th century to the beginning of this century it was used as a hospital. The clinic was then moved to a new building the Hospital de Santa Creu i de Sant Pau (*see*

The bust of Dr Fleming

Casa Bruno Quadros

Rose window, Santa Maria del Pi

page 52). Today the old hospital building is home to the university medical faculty and central library. Behind the Gothic facade is a Gothic inner courtyard, with a pleasantly peaceful atmosphere. Exhibitions are held in the hospital chapel.

On the north side of the grounds is the tranquil Plaça Dr Fleming. At fiesta time the inhabitants of the El Raval district gather around the bust of the co-discoverer of penicillin (1881–1955). As in the past, El Raval is one of the poorest districts in the city but undergoing radical changes.

Going back to the Ramblas, you will see an enormous, emblem-like mosaic by Joan Miró in the middle of the avenue. On festival days the *sardana* is danced here (*see page 81*). The **Casa Bruno Quadros** on the north side of the Rambla sets the architectural tone here. This comical house, complete with both a dragon and an umbrella, is from the last century and stands at the cross-roads of Carrer Boqueria and the narrow Carrer Cardenal Casañas. The latter leads to the ★★ **Plaça del Pi**, one of the most beautiful squares in the whole city, where buskers often perform on account of the excellent acoustics. Pretty facades are to be seen on the richly decorated artisan's house, the Ganiveteria Josep Roca, on the Farmàcia del Pi (still in excellent condition) and on the Estamperia (from 1789). Although the latter no longer has stamps for sale, you can buy original postcards and all types of prints. The most striking building, however, is the ★ **Santa Maria del Pi** church. This was built between 1322 and 1453, although historical records also document a church in the 10th century in a new district outside the earlier medieval city. The west side of the church has an enormous **rose window** over the main entrance, one of the largest of the Catalan-Gothic style. The church was restored after being damaged in the civil war. Inside, the beautiful glass paintings mute the incoming light. The tomb of the 18th-century painter Antoni Viladomat is particularly interesting.

On the west side of the square is the entrance to the Galeries Maldà, a shopping arcade which goes as far as Carrer Portaferrissa, and also has a way through to the Carrer del Pi. Boutiques and jewellery shops are the most prominent features of this tempting labyrinth.

Plaça del Pi merges into Plaça de Sant Josep Oriol, with its memorial to the dramatist Àngel Guimerà (1847–1924), who was extremely popular during his lifetime. On Saturday and Sunday there is a market for painters and artists around the memorial. The Bar del Pi is a popular meeting point both for locals and tourists, with the attraction of being able to sit out in front of the bar, either in the sun or in the shadow of the plane trees.

Going back to the Rambla dels Caputxins, on the corner of Carrer de Sant Pau is the opera house, the ★★ **Gran**

Teatre del Liceu ❽, which was built in 1845. Shortly after its completion it burned down (in 1861), but was immediately renovated and acquired an international reputation.

Customers at the Café de l'Opera

The opera house

21

In 1994 another fire devastated the building, but immediate rebuilding plans included expansion of the site as well as complete restoration. It is due to open in 1999 with vastly improved stage facilities, making it possible to present two operas at once. Tickets from servicaixa or the theatre, tel: 93 485 9913.

The upper-class visitors to the opera were given a fright in 1893 when the anarchist Salvador French threw two bombs into the 'high temple of the bourgeoisie' during the second act of Rossini's *William Tell* opera. Little damage was done, however, and world-famous tenors continued to perform their arias in the magnificent atmosphere of the theatre.

Opposite the opera house is a small art nouveau café, which takes its name from the temple of the muses: the Café de l'Opera. As in the past, people meet here to discuss life over a cup of coffee, to write or just to observe the local scene. And they stay well into the night.

From the Gran Teatre it's worth making a detour to the Carrer de Sant Pau. This leads right into the heart of the poverty, prostitution and child-criminality of the famous – or rather infamous – Barri Xinès. The street, and indeed the whole district, is extremely lively, with countless small shops and, above all, bars, where a very mixed clientele meets at all hours of the day. After about 15 minutes you will reach ★ **Sant Pau del Camp** ❾.

Sant Pau del Camp

The addition of the words *del camp* comes from the fact that when it was built (around 1000) this Romanesque church was situated in the fields outside the city wall. Neglected for a long time, and even used as military barracks around the turn of the century, the church and the surrounding buildings of the former Benedictine monastery have been restored to their former elegance and splendour. The entrance portal, dating from 1120 and the Romanesque cloister are especially worth seeing. It is one of the few cloisters with trefoil arches. Mythical creatures and biblical figures decorate the capitals, along with plant and abstract designs.

Biblical figure

Continuing further west from the church is the formerly magnificent boulevard **Paral.lel**. Today there are numerous cinemas, theatres, variety shows and dance halls, and the street is particularly interesting at night (*see page 90*).

On the way back to the Ramblas turn off into Carrer Sant Roman and visit the Marsella Bar, infamous for its absinthe – and local colour. Continue down Carrer Nou de la Rambla, and on the right is the ★★ **Palau Güell** ⑩ (Nos 3–5). This palace with its mighty balcony over the entrance is one of the first works which Gaudí constructed for his patron, Count Güell (*see page 77*). It was built in 1888 and Gaudí's instructions were to create a building which would serve not only as living quarters but also as a venue for exhibitions and other events. For all this Gaudí had only 18m (60ft) by 22m (72ft) at his disposal. He solved the problem brilliantly. The ground floor was designed as a large room, with the minimum of columns, and served as a reception area. Situated at the back was a stable for the horses. The middle floor has a centrally-located salon with an organ. Around the stairs on the upper floor are a number of small living rooms and bedrooms. Gaudí was also responsible for the building's interior decoration, and the wooden and metal decorations are particularly impressive.

Gaudí's Palau Güell

Opposite Carrer Nou de la Rambla a short street (Carrer Colom) leads directly to the ★★ **Plaça Reial**. The 'royal square' is a harmonious collection of buildings, which were constructed in 1848 by architect Daniel Molina on the site of a former Capuchin monastery. The classical buildings with their wide arcade passageways, the palms, the fountains in the middle of the square, and, last but not least, the lanterns which Gaudí designed in 1878–79 all contribute to the wonderful atmosphere of the square. Both during the day and in the evening most of the numerous cafés and restaurants in the arcades are full, whilst musicians and artists use the square as their stage. On Sunday morning, stamps and coins are offered for sale, whilst at night pickpockets and drug dealers go about their business amongst the crowds. This explains the presence of a police car, where thefts can be reported.

Plaça Reial

Beginning more or less at the Plaça Reial is the **Rambla Santa Mònica**. On the left hand side, at the Plaça

In the Rambla Santa Mònica

del Teatre, is a memorial to the dramatist and founder of modern Catalan theatre, Frederic Soler (1839–1895), who also wrote under the pseudonym Serafí Pitarra. On the opposite side of the street stands the Teatre Principal. It has been used for productions since 1603. In 1568 King Philip II gave his permission to the Hospital de la Santa Creu to build a stage, so that they could use the proceeds to finance the costs of the hospital. The present building is from the 19th century, and various alterations have been undertaken since then.

23

The pedestrian avenue now becomes wider and offers space for all kinds of extraordinary activities: fortune tellers read Tarot cards, a gypsy reads palms and coffee grains, a painter will do your portrait in 15 minutes, and shoe-cleaners offer their services. If you are suffering from stress you can even get your blood pressure measured at a small table. Every weekend there is a craft-work market at the lower end of the Rambla Santa Mònica (Saturday afternoon, Sunday all day). At night the street becomes a catwalk for prostitutes, transvestites, homosexuals and the homeless. One should try to avoid the narrow streets to the northeast of the Rambla. Theft is not just possible here, it is quite probable.

On the right hand side of the Rambla Santa Mònica is the **Centre d'Art Santa Mònica ⓫**, situated in the rooms of a former 17th-century monastery. Exhibitions are regularly shown here. Opposite, a decorated entrance booth indicates the way to an entertaining attraction, the **Museu de Cera ⓬** . The wax-figure museum, housed in a building dating from 1867 which is still in good condition, includes lifelike models of famous personalities from the worlds of art and politics. Light and sound effects are so cleverly used that visitors will often have the impression that the personalities are standing in the flesh in front of them. (Monday to Friday 10am–1.30pm and

Figure in the Museu de Cera

4.30–7.30pm (all day during the high season); Saturday and Sunday 10am–8pm.)

The Ramblas feed into the Plaça del Portal de la Pau. In the middle of the square, used by tens of thousands of cars each day, is a bronze monument standing more than 50m (160ft) high. This is the ★ **Monument a Colom** ⓭, the Columbus Monument, erected by Gaietà Buigas in 1888 in memory of the visit to Barcelona of the great seafarer and discoverer of America. He was received by King Ferdinand II in 1483 in the Saló del Tinell (*see page 28*), at the end of his first voyage. Inside the monument a lift leads up to a viewing platform. From here there is a fantastic view over the harbour, the Ramblas and, to the west, to Tibidabo. All in all, an excellent place to get a general overview of the city.

Columbus points the way

If the Columbus Monument whets your appetite for things maritime, visit the nearby museum which has wonderful exhibits covering all aspects of sea travel. This is the ★ **Museu Marítim**, housed in the huge wave-like covered halls of the Reials Drassanes, the 13th-century royal shipyards. The ships in which Catalan seafarers conquered the Mediterranean in the 14th and 15th centuries were built here. The exhibits include small models, life-size replicas, sea maps (for example from Amerigo Vespucci, 1439), documents, nautical instruments and galleon figures. Renovated in 1995, the museum now includes an exciting interactive exhibition about life at sea in the past and present.

A good way to finish off this route is to take a coffee or snack in one of the many cafés on the Ramblas or on the harbour promenade, Moll de la Fusta, north of the Columbus Monument (*Route 3*). Alternatively, take a trip on a *Golondrina* (literally, a swallow), as the harbour boats are called.

Galera Real in the Museu Marítim

Route 2

Barri Gòtic

This route goes into the Gothic Quarter, the area where Barcelona's history began when the Iberian Laietani tribe arrived. Next to settle were the Romans and the two main roads of their settlement – cardus (from northwest to southeast, today Carrer Bisbe Irurita/Ciutat) and decumanus (from northeast to southwest) – still form the main axes of this district on the Mons Taber hill. Later, Visigothic, medieval and Gothic buildings were erected here, dominated by the magnificent Santa Eulàlia Cathedral. Allow at least half a day for this journey through history.

The circular walk begins at Plaça Nova. Picasso designed the facade of the building which houses the Association of Architects, using a simple fresco (1962). Through the **Portal Bisbe** – framed by two Roman towers which are remains of the 4th-century city wall – you come to the area which is steeped in history. On the right is the **Palau Episcopal ⑭**. The first bishops' palace was built as early as 926, and was given its current form in the 12th century. In 1784 the facade on the Plaça Nova was extended. Entrance is usually permitted to the inner courtyard with its Romanesque arcades and windows framed by stone decorations (12th–14th centuries).

The church of Sant Felip Neri

25

Plaça de Sant Felip Neri

Continuing down the Carrer del Bisbe, there is a small square after a few metres, Garriga i Bachs. The square is dominated by a memorial to the Napoleonic Wars, which was designed by the artists Josep Llimona and Vincenç Navarro. On the right the narrow Carrer Montjuïc del Bisbe leads to the idyllic ★ **Plaça de Sant Felip Neri**. Seventeenth-century buildings are grouped around a fountain whilst a plane tree offers shade. Amongst the buildings is the Sant Felip Neri church. The square is extremely atmospheric and peaceful, at least when the children from the nearby school are not running around and playing football against the walls of the houses. But it was not so peaceful during the civil war. Public executions took place here and bullet holes can still be seen in the walls. In the Middle Ages the square was the centre of the Jewish Quarter (the *Call, see page 27*). On the eastern side of the square the former shoemakers' guildhall is now home to the **Museu del Calçat Antic ⑮**, the Antique Shoe Museum, whose exhibits include the largest shoe in the world, made for the Columbus Monument, as well as

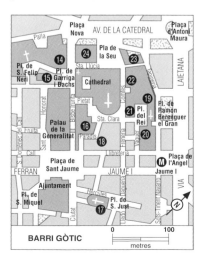

a number of interesting Roman specimens. (Tuesday to Saturday 11.30am–2pm.) Via the Carrer Sant Felip Neri and Carrer Sant Sever, the route leads back to the Carrer del Bisbe. This narrow street between the facade of the Palau de la Generalitat on the right (with a relief of Saint George from 1418 by Pere Johan) and the **Casa dels Canonges** ⑯ goes under a neo-Gothic crossing which was added in 1928.

The spacious square ★★ **Plaça de Sant Jaume** has its roots in a Roman forum, where the main streets of the city joined together. Today it is the focal point for Barcelona's political life. Facing each other, and watched over by friendly uniformed guards, are the two power centres of the city and the region: the Ajuntament (town hall) on the east side of the square and on the west side the ★ **Palau de la Generalitat de Catalunya**, seat of the autonomous government of Catalonia. Particularly spectacular is the architecture of the palace's 15th-century ★ **inner courtyards**. The main facade was built somewhat later, at the beginning of the 17th century. Delicate Gothic arcades surround the first courtyard on the upper floor. From here you come to the Gothic Sant Jordi chapel (16th-century) and the Pati dels Tarongers, the Orange Tree Patio (1532). From here a delightful Renaissance door leads into the Saló de Sant Jordi (16th-century), which originally served as a chapel. The majesty of the Saló Daurat conference hall, with its splendid golden coffered ceiling, reflects the power of the Catalan parliament which has existed since the Middle Ages.

Opposite the seat of the state parliament and almost as impressive is the **Casa de la Ciutat**. The oldest part of the house, which can only be seen from the Carrer de la Ciutat, dates from the 14th century. Behind the classical 19th-century facade with its large balconies is the

Enjoying the sun

Casa de la Ciutat interior…
… and exterior

mayor's office. He holds his meetings in the ★ **Saló de Cent**. This lovely domed hall, with a marble floor and its walls painted in the national colours of red and yellow, is from the 15th century. Equally spectacular is the banqueting hall, Saló de les Cròniques, designed in 1928 by the famous Catalan painter Josep Maria Sert, who also decorated the cathedral in Vic. Scenes from 14th-century Catalan oriental expeditions are portrayed. On the ground floor of the Ajuntament on the left near the main entrance is a city information office.

Both the Palau de la Generalitat and the town hall can only be visited occasionally and only after making an arrangement by phone (details in the city hall). On one special day in the year both buildings are open to the general public: 23 April, Saint George's day, the day of Catalonia's patron saint (*see page 80*).

Next to and behind the building of the Generalitat in the Middle Ages was the ★ **Jewish Quarter** or *Call*. This quarter stretched roughly from Carrer del Call to Carrer Banys Nous in the south and the Carrer Palla in the west. In the narrow Carrer Marlet (the continuation of Carrer Fruita), at No 1, there is still a plaque with Hebrew inscriptions dating from 692. The Jewish community was highly respected for centuries and had considerable influence on public life in the city and particularly on the economy. During the reign of Jaume I in the middle of the 13th century, the first anti-Jewish sentiments were expressed. (For example, the Spanish Jews had to wear special clothes.) Later they were held responsible for having brought the plague and at the end of the 14th century the synagogues were closed or converted into churches and the materials were used for public buildings. In 1424 the Jews had to leave the city.

Nowadays there is a plethora of small shops and businesses in the narrow lanes of the old Jewish Quarter. Particularly abundant are household goods and jewellery shops, which mainly sell cheap costume jewellery to wholesalers, who then sell it on to the public at the little stands in and around the Ramblas.

To the east of the town hall, the Carrer d'Hèrcules leads to a church which is sadly all too often overlooked. The **Sant Just i Pastor church** is the oldest in the city. Its current form, however, dates back only to the 18th century. Up to the 15th century, church services were held here for the royal family, who only had a few steps to go from their nearby residence at the Plaça del Rei. Because of its intimate atmosphere Sant Just i Pastor is now very popular for weddings, particularly at weekends. Inside there are impressive stoops and the Retablo de San Felix from 1525. If there is enough time, it is worth stopping for a quick snack at the Café de l'Academia, with its view

Hebrew inscription in the Jewish Quarter

27

Altar in Sant Just i Pastor

Cake shop on Carrer Llibreteria

Medieval Plaça del Rei

The Saló de Tinell

of the square and fountain (1367). As an alternative, head in the direction of the port and visit a bar in Carrer Lledó or Carrer Regomir.

From Plaça Sant Just the route leads via Carrer Dagueria to **Carrer Llibreteria**. Numerous excellent cake shops can be found in this street, along with the Cereria Subir'á. This candle shop at No 7 has a long tradition, and no doubt profits from its proximity to so many churches. It sells every possible type of candle, as well as comical wax products. Heading towards the Plaça Sant Jaume a good place for a break is at Barcelona's smallest café: Meson del Café at No 16 has standing room only, but serves excellent coffee in a rustic atmosphere. Continuing on, you come to the Carrer Paradis on the right. Here there is a milestone marking the highest point on Mons Taber (*see page 25*). On the second corner of the street, hidden in the building of the *Centre Excursionista de Catalunya* (the walkers' club), are some of the oldest and most beautiful of the ruins left over from the Roman epoch in Barcelona. Four enormous columns from a former **Temple of Augustus ⓲** (around AD100) are squeezed into a small inner courtyard. The best view can be had from the gallery on the first floor.

At the end of Carrer Paradis the Baixada de Santa Clara leads to the right to one of the most impressive squares in the city, the ★★ **Plaça del Rei**. The 'square of the kings' is surrounded by dignified medieval buildings and has wonderful acoustics. Theatrical and musical events are held here in summer. The Mirador del Rei Martí, which towers over the square, used to be a watchtower. At the northern corner, a wide staircase leads up to the **Palau Reial Major ⓳**, once the residence of the counts of Barcelona and later of the kings of Aragón. The inside of the vault in the enormous throne room is particularly impressive. The 36-m (120-ft) long ★ **Saló de Tinell**, built between 1356 and 1370, was used not only for splendid receptions, but also as a court room for the bloody Spanish Inquisition. From the anteroom of the throne room the way leads to the 14th-century Santa Àgata chapel. Here is the *Retrat del Conestable*, an altarpiece by the important Catalan painter Jaume Huguet (1414–92).

The chapel is connected by a staircase to the 15th-century Palau Clariana Padellàs. Originally this stood in Carrer de Mercaders. However, it was in the path of a planned new street and in 1931 was dismantled brick by brick and moved to the Plaça del Rei. Today it houses the ★★**Museu d'Història de la Ciutat ⓴** (main entrance Carrer Veguer). On the lower floor of the museum, visitors go through the excavations from Barcelona's earliest times, which stretch as far as the cathedral. Among the exhibits are the foundations from the first city walls and from houses, statues, mosaics and various objects from the Roman, early-Christian and Visigothic periods. Silos, bathing areas, parts of Roman forums, a 4th-century early-Christian basilica and the 11th-century Romanesque cathedral can all be seen side by side here. In the three upper floors exhibits from the city's history up to as late as the 19th century are on display. (Monday 3.30–8pm, Tuesday to Saturday 9am–8pm, Sunday 9am–1.30pm.)

Go back to the Plaça del Rei and a short distance down Baixada Santa Clara, before turning right into Carrer dels Comtes de Barcelona, directly on the right is the **Palau del Lloctinent** ㉑. The former 'palace of the representative' is a splendid 16th-century late-Gothic building. Today the archive of the house of Aragón is housed here in the rooms around the harmoniously designed inner courtyard, with its fountain and colonnaded gallery. The collection contains documents from the royal chancellery and papers relating to international treaties and questions of fiefdom. Some date back as far as the 9th century. The inner courtyard can be visited but special permission is needed to get into the archive.

A few metres further on, in the former Palace of the Inquisition, is the ★★ **Museu Frederic Marès** ㉒. The art collection here comes from a donation made by the sculptor Frederic Marés i Deulovol in 1940. In keeping with the interests of the donor, it includes an excellent collection of sculptures from the late Middle Ages to the 19th century. Also on display on the three floors are crucifixes, altars and holy pictures. One particularly interesting section is the Museu Sentimental on the third floor. Here there are various everyday objects from the past two centuries, including braces, walking sticks, keys, matchboxes, umbrellas and glasses. (Tuesday to Saturday 9am–2pm, 4–7pm, Sunday 9am–2pm.)

Museu Frederic Mares

29

Palace courtyard

In the **palace courtyard** on the right is an entrance to the excavations of the Museu d'Història de la Ciutat (*see page 28*). From the back of the courtyard there is an excellent view over the narrow Carrer Tapineria (*see below*). The small square in front of the museum and the Romanesque side-portals of the cathedral (*see below*) are both memorials to Saint Ives, *Sant Iu* in Catalan.

A few metres further on, the narrow lane opens up into the spacious cathedral square. In the corner on the right is the **Casa de la Pia Almoina** ㉓. This building, also known as the Casa de la Canonja, was built in 935 as the home of its founder. From 1009 the name Casa de la Pia Almoina became commonly used, because a charitable organisation distributed food from here to the needy. Now housing the Museu Diocesà, various exhibitions are held here.

The southwestern border of the Pla de la Seu is formed by the **Casa de l'Ardiaca** ㉔. This late-Gothic house with

Renaissance elements stands on a Romanesque foundation. It was used as a residence by the archdeacons, and later become the home of the Chamber of Lawyers. In 1919 the city's archive was transferred here. The inner courtyard is idyllic, with an old palm tree and a Gothic fountain, where the 'egg-dance' (*l'ou com balla*) is performed on Corpus Christi (*see page 80*).

Allow enough time to visit the building which dominates all others on the Roman Mons Taber, the mighty ★★★ **Cathedral** (**Catedral La Seu**) which is dedicated to Saint Eulàlia, the female patron saint of Barcelona.

Barcelona Cathedral

Originally a Visigothic basilica stood on this site, but it was destroyed by the Arabs in the 8th century. A Romanesque church was then erected on the foundations; parts still remain at the northeastern Sant Iu Portal. The basic elements of today's cathedral, including the two towers at the back, were built between 1298 and 1448. The main facade, however, is relatively new, only dating back to 1892. The dome itself wasn't finished until 1913. Although based on old Gothic plans, the new Gothic elements appear somewhat out of place and not part of a homogenous style. But this in no way reduces the bombastic appearance of the western facade.

The main portal is richly decorated with biblical scenes and figures. Inside, the stained glass windows, some of which date back to the 15th century, are situated high up on the walls and allow in only the dimmest of light. The interior – 83m (270ft) long, 37m (120ft) wide and 25m (80ft) high – is spanned by a ribbed vault. On the right is Capella del Santíssim, the largest of a total of 29 chapels. It houses a crucifix which has turned black from the smoke of countless candles. It is said that Don John of Austria took this crucifix with him to the battle of Lepanto in 1571.

The Gothic portal

The tomb of Saint Olegarius (died 1136) is also here.

One feature which is very typical of the Spanish Gothic style is the choir, which is situated in the middle of the nave, and which is closed off at the side and at the back. On the outside are reliefs from the 16th century by the sculptors Ordóñez and Villar. These reliefs portray the suffering of Saint Eulàlia. The Gothic ornamentation of the choir stall is from the 15th and 16th centuries. Whether of plants or people, they are extremely vivid and expressive. In front of the high altar, whose top is supported by Visigothic capitals, steps lead into the crypt. Here there is a white Italian marble sarcophagus (1327) containing the mortal remains of Saint Eulàlia. She died as a martyr in 304. In the chapels of the choir area there are wonderful wing altars and sarcophagi, including that of Bishop Ramon d'Escales (1386–98) in the first chapel on the left.

Cathedral service

The sacristy on the southern side contains the extensive church treasures, which can only be visited with special permission. They include the silver throne of King Martí, and the mass book of Saint Eulàlia. The Porta de San Sever leads to the impressive ★ **cloister**. It is surrounded by numerous small chapels, in which the church patrons and wealthy citizens have put up memorials. In the middle is a garden with palms and magnolia trees. On Corpus Christi an egg is put on the water of the fountain, much like the ceremony in the Casa de l'Ardiaca (*see page 30*). There are no legends to explain this ritual. In earlier times the geese warded off thieves and other intruders with their loud cackling. On the western side of the cloister is the Museu de la Catedral. Among its precious exhibits are a 15th-century altarpiece by Jaume Huguet (*see page 28*) and a late-Gothic Pietà (1490) by the painter Bartolomé Bermejo. (Monday to Sunday 11am–1pm.)

31

The cloister has three exits. The Porta de la Pietat, which is of Gothic origin and has a Flemish wood relief in the tympanum, leads to Baixada Santa Clara. The Porta de Santa Eulàlia, with its figure of the Saint in the tympanum, opens up into the Carrer del Bisbe Irurita. The third way of leaving the cloister is via the Romanesque Capella de Santa Llúcia (1268), where many of the faithful still pray at times when no church service is being held.

On Saturday at around 6.30pm and on Sunday at noon melodic music can be heard from the Pla de la Seu, when the *sardana* is danced (*see page 81*).

To complete the walk, go down Carrer Tapineria. This 'street of the cobblers' leads straight along the city wall to the **Plaça de Berenguer el Gran.** A small garden area has been created around the bronze statue of Count Ramon Berenguer III. From here you can once more appreciate the beauty of the Barri Gòtic. Beyond the ruins of the old city wall, the Capella de Santa Àgata, the Martí tower and the silhouette of the cathedral can all be seen.

Count Ramon Berenguer III

Route 3

The Port and La Ribera

For decades Barcelona neglected its waterfront. Cut off from the old city by the four lanes of the Passeig de Colom, the port district was a sleepy and unappealing area. It is only in recent years that considerable effort has been made to make the part of the city covered by Route 3 more attractive. This route also goes into the Ribera district, which was full of life in the Middle Ages, but was seriously damaged – and in some areas razed to the ground – after 1714 by Philip V. At least three hours should be allowed for the tour. For those with more time, a walk through Barceloneta can be added on; from Plaça Antoni López it is only a short stroll to the fishing quarters, where you relax on the city's beach or in one of the many fish restaurants. The route begins at the Plaça Portal de la Pau.

Taking in the view

32

From the viewing platform of ★ **Monument a Colom**, the Columbus Monument (*see page 24*), there is a splendid view over Spain's largest Mediterranean port. In the southwest the industrial harbour stretches around to the site of the SEAT works. This subsidiary of the German VW company has developed into one of the largest employers in the city. Nearby is the Moll de Barcelona, the pier for the ferries which go to Mallorca and the other Balearic islands twice a day in the high season. Right next to the Columbus column is a neo-classical building which houses the port authority and is one of the symbols of the prosperity and power of the city around the turn of the century.

Golondrinas

The Port Vell from the Columbus monument

By the landing steps in front of the port authority building are the *Golondrinas*. Every 20 minutes from 11am–8.30pm these small passenger boats chug round the harbour; round trips to the Olympic Harbour depart at 11am, 1pm and 4pm. To the left of the old landing steps a wood

walkway stretches across the mouth of the **Port Vell**, the old port where the city's two yacht clubs are based. Walk across here to the Moll d'Espanya and the Maremagnum complex of shops, restaurants and cinemas, to the ★ **Aquarium** (10am–10pm in summer, 10am–9pm in winter), which has an excellent display of Mediterranean sea life, with walkways leading underwater among sharks and rays. The jetty that leads back to the main quay provides a view across to the Barceloneta fishing fleet and the leisure port, where the Palau de Mar is a good place to eat and also houses a museum of Catalan history. The main quay from here to the Columbus monument is the **Moll de la Fusta**, a pleasant place for a stroll.

Moll de la Fusta

Life is quieter on the other side of the Passeig de Colom. The **Carrer Ample**, which runs parallel to the Passeig de Colom, was once home to the city's richest inhabitants, before they moved to Eixample in the 19th century (*see page 75*). Today the street is inhabited by workers and artisans, with lots of little shops. The tranquil, tree-lined **Plaça Duc de Medinaceli**, with its monument of Catalan admiral Galceran Marquet, still gives some impression of the former glory of the street.

Bar in Carrer Ample

A little further north a number of houses have been demolished in order to create a clear view of the ★ **Església de la Mercè** . The Madonna sculpture on the dome can be seen from far away, and the church itself is dedicated to the Virgin de la Mercè, the second patron saint of the city, following Santa Eulàlia. Building began in 1267 and a further monastery was added in the 17th century. Soon afterwards the church was renovated in baroque style. When the nuns had to leave in 1835, the king's governors moved in. The interior of the present-day parish church (c 1775) still radiates its baroque splendour.

Statue adorning La Llotja

Both Carrer Ample and Passeig de Colom lead to the Plaça Antoni López (1910), which bears the name of the founder of the *Transatlantic* shipping line. The appearance of the square is dominated by the Correus i Telègrafs building, the main post office which was built around the turn of the century. To the north, between Passeig Isabell II, Plaça del Palau and Carrer del Consulat is the protruding building of the old stock exchange, ★ **La Llotja** . This building, parts of which date back to the 14th century, was originally the headquarters of the Consolat del Mar, an institution which was responsible for regulating trade and sea-traffic. At the end of the 18th century the whole complex was renovated to form a harmonious whole. The main facade faces the Plaça del Palau. From here you can walk through to the romantic inner courtyard. The highlight of the whole complex, however, is the large 14th-century Gothic hall and the classical premises of the former stock exchange.

Passeig Isabel II in the Porxos Xifré

Set Portes Restaurant

Another nearby complex on Passeig Isabel II, recognisable by its beautiful arcade, is the **Porxos Xifré 28**. This was built by the banker Josep Xifré who had made his fortune in America at the beginning of the 19th century. He commissioned the building, with its seven portals, after returning to his home city in the middle of the century. He even managed to reach the position of mayor of Barcelona. Today the building is home to a strange mixture of businesses. On the side facing Passeig Isabel II is the posh **Set Portes Restaurant** (*see page 85*), whilst on the harbour side, in Carrer Reina Cristina, there are bazaars and little shops selling masses of electronic items from the Far East. As well as clocks, computers and video recorders, however, the street can also offer a culinary jewel which is in stark contrast to the noble atmosphere of the Set Portes. The whole district meets in **Can Paixano**, a small, and from the outside not particularly striking, place. *Bocadillos* or *entrepans* (sandwiches) can be eaten here – standing up, of course. To drink there is *cava* (sparkling wine, *see page 72*), and the prices are very reasonable indeed. With its uncleaned walls, tables to stand at, hectic waiters and the smell of wine and cheese, sold in one corner to take away, Can Paixano has a fantastic atmosphere and is one of the most famous meeting places in the city.

The walk continues along the Avinguda Marquès de L'Argentera, past the neo-classical building of the Gobierno Civil – the seat of the civil government subordinate to Madrid – to the Estació de França. This stylish 19th-century railway station with its wood panelling and marble floors, was given an extensive facelift before the 1992 Olympic Games. It is a terminal for national and international long-distance trains. A little further along, the Passeig de la Circumval.lació turns off to the right.

It leads south around the Parc de la Ciutadella, to become the main street leading to the Olympic village (*see page 39*) and the Olympic harbour.

At the end of the Avinguda Marquès de l'Argentera, is the massive wrought-iron entrance to the ★ **Parc de la Ciutadella**. Visitors are greeted by a statue of General Prim on horseback. In 1869 the general handed over the citadel which Philip V had built 150 years earlier to the people of the city to be demolished. Only the buildings of the former arsenal remain standing, and the Catalan Parliament meets there today.

Housed in the spacious rooms of a nearby building is the **Museu d'Art Modern** (MNAC) **㉙** . This is less a museum of modern or contemporary art than a display of works primarily by Catalan artists from between 1830 and 1950 (including Marià Fortuny, Josep Maria Sert and Miquel Blay).

Museu d'Art Modern

One section is devoted to fabulous jewellery and furniture from the modernist period, and illustrations and caricatures by local artists, especially Ramón Casas, are on show in a number of halls. (Tuesday to Saturday 9am–7.30pm, Sunday and public holidays 9am–2pm.)

In the southern part of the 30-hectacre (75-acre) park is the **Zoo** which opened in 1892. (9.30am–7pm, winter 10am–5pm.) The main attractions are the primates, the *Aquarama*, where whales and dolphins perform, and the children's zoo where younger members of the family can touch the animals.

Dolphins in the Zoo's Aquarama

A **cascading fountain** **㉚** occupies a central place in the park. Below an impressive four-horsed chariot, and surrounded by dragons, a waterfall pours into an attractively designed pond. It is also possible to take out rowing boats here. The fountain was a joint effort by a number of Catalan artists, including Antoni Gaudí. Gaudí was a colleague of the landscape gardener Josep Fontseré i Mestres, the man responsible for landscaping the whole park for the Universal Exposition which took place here in 1888. He also had the idea of exhibiting sculptures by famous artists in the park. This included the fountain statue of a lady with an umbrella by Roig i Soler, and the female figures *El Desconsol* (Desperation) by Josep Llimona, in the pond in front of the parliament building.

The **Castell dels Tres Dragons** **㉛** by the western gate was also created for the exposition, and was designed by art nouveau architect Domènech i Montaner. This richly decorated sandstone castle housed the exposition restaurant and is now home of the Zoological Museum (Museu Zoològic). (Tuesday to Saturday 9am–2pm.) Right next to the castle are two buildings which form a complete architectural contrast to the castle: the glass pavilion (Hivernacle) – a romantic iron construction from the end of the

19th century, which is nowadays used for exhibitions and open-air concerts – and the Geology Museum (Museu Geològic). (Tuesday to Saturday 9am–2pm.)

Outside the park, around 300m to the west on Passeig Lluís Companys, the **Arc de Triomf** ㉜ can be seen clearly. This was designed by modernist Josep Vilaseca in Mudéjar style. In 1888 this gigantic brick arch served as the entrance to the site of the Universal Exposition.

The Arc de Triomf

Leaving the park by the gate near the Zoological Museum leads to the newly-designed Passeig de Picasso. This formerly rather dreary street has been livened up with an artistically-designed pond and a glass cube sculpture in honour of Picasso by contemporary painter and sculptor Antoni Tàpies. After going a few metres in the direction of the port, turn right into Carrer Fusina. Here the **Art-Cava de Fusina** offers a peaceful, stress-free atmosphere where you can relax. It is a meeting point for artists and students, whose pictures are also exhibited on the walls. On the left hand side is the **Mercat del Born** ㉝, an enormous, beautiful 19th-century iron structure, formerly Barcelona's main market. A few years ago there were plans to pull it down, but by popular demand it survived and its future is under discussion.

Art-Cava de Fusina

36

Via Plaça Comercial the route leads to **Passeig del Born**. Barcelonans can still enjoy peace in this square, which was one of the city's main meeting points in the Middle Ages. Undisturbed by the hurly-burly of the nearby Ramblas, the locals sit on benches, gossip about their neighbours and just enjoy life. Plenty of little bars, restaurants and contemporary art galleries in the side streets offer the opportunity to while away the time, both during the day and in the evenings. The southern side of the square is dominated by the giant buttresses of Santa Maria del Mar, one of the most beautiful churches in the city. Go round the left-hand side to a small cobbled square, where the children of the district play. In former times the Fossar de les Moreres cemetery was situated here, where those who fell in the battle of 1714 (*see page 11*) were buried. There is a marble monument in memory of the fallen.

Passeig del Born

From Plaça Santa Maria the ★ **Església Santa Maria del Mar** ㉞ with its two mighty towers, appears to be a fortress. The church was built in just 50 years (1323–78) under the direction of architect Berenguer de Montagut. As a result it has an astonishing unity of style. The most striking feature from the outside is the enormous rose window over the main entrance, whose stained glass only reveals its brilliance from the inside, particularly in the light of the midday sun. Inside the three-aisled basilica – whose building materials came from a quarry on Montjuïc – the stained-glass windows (some from the 15th century) and the crypt under the baroque **altar** are especially interesting. The treasures of this modern day parish can also be visited, although many items disappeared during the civil war.

Santa Maria del Mar, altar

Now go back down Carrer Sombrerers (hatters – many streets in the area are named after the medieval guilds) – and you will come to ★ **Carrer Montcada.** In this former patrician street there are numerous wonderful palaces: Palau Dalmases (No 20, 15th century); Palau Cervelló (No 25, 15th century) and the Palau de Llió (No 12, 16th century). Here the Museu de Tèxtil i de la Indumentària (Textile Museum) displays clothing and other items covering five centuries. Enjoy a coffee in its patio or browsing in the shop. (Tuesday to Saturday 9am–2pm, 4.30–7pm; Sunday, public holidays 9am–2pm.)

The buildings in Carrer Montcada are full of history, and many now house public offices. But there are also numerous well-known galleries (for example, Galerie Maeght at No 25) and arty shops. And the street also caters for culinary interests. In the Xampanyet bar (No 22), sparkling wine is served from lemonade bottles, along with all kinds of delicious titbits, and nearby is a typical Basque bar.

The main attraction and lifeblood of Carrer Montcada, however, has for many years been a museum which is situated in two palaces, the Palau Aguilar (No 15, 13th century) and Palau Baró de Castellet (No 178, 15th century). This is the ★★★ **Museu Picasso** ㉟. Born in Málaga, Pablo Picasso (1881–1973) studied painting in Barcelona as a young man. He painted in the Escuela de Bellas Artes, which was in the La Llotja stock exchange (*see page 33*), and where his father was a teacher. Picasso was often to be found with his clique of friends in the Quatre Gats (*see page 86*) and the Ramblas district. His famous cubist painting *Les Demoiselles d'Avignon* (1907) is said to have been created in Carrer Avinyó.

Pablo Picasso

On his death Picasso bequeathed a number of his works to the city. These were joined by the collection of Jaume Sabartés, a friend and secretary of Picasso, and the Planduria collection, which was bought by the city. All in all the museum has over 3,600 of the artist's works, of which over 500 are on display. One room is devoted specially to his graphic and ceramic works. (Tuesday to Saturday 10am–8pm, Sunday 10am–3pm.) Adjoining the museum is the Café del Museu where one can enjoy a coffee or meal, and an excellent postcard and poster shop. Good travelling exhibitions are also held here.

From the Picasso museum it is only a short distance to the Carrer de la Princesa, a pleasant place to take a stroll on account of its interesting little shops. At **El Rey de la Magia** (No 11) you will find yourself transported to a magical world. Cross Via Laietana to Jaune I which leads to

El Rey de la Magia

the Plaça de Sant Jaume (*see page 26*). Anyone who still has the time and energy to keep going should cross Carrer de la Princesa, continue straight on and amble through the business districts of Santa Caterina and Sant Pere. Going past the Mercat Santa Caterina ㊱ (Avinguda Fr. Cambó) leads on to the ★ **Palau de la Música Catalana** ㊲ (Carrer Sant Pere Més Alt, *see page 56*).

Barceloneta

Up until the beginning of the 18th century this district in the eastern part of the city was only inhabited by a few fishermen. It first took on its present-day form after 1714. Philip V had captured Barcelona and planned to build a large fortress complex (Ciutadella) in the Ribera district. To this end 52 streets and over 1,200 houses were razed to the ground in this densely populated area. The French engineer, Prosper de Verboom, was then commissioned to build a new residential district in a previously unbuilt beach area. The construction of Little Barcelona didn't begin until 1753, with streets laid out to cross each other at right angles. The houses were originally only two floors high, but have since extended upwards into the heavens. The blocks of flats, which were very modern for their time, attracted the residents of Ribera, as well as fishermen and sailors. Soon a district with its own special atmosphere grew up. There are many first-class restaurants on Passeig Nacional (now Joan de Borbó), which stretches along the harbour from Plaça de Pau Vila to Torre Sant Sebastià, the tower for the cable car to Montjuïc.

38

Attractive restaurant

Turning left from the Passeig into Carrer Escuder, you will come to Plaça Barceloneta where there are more restaurants and bars. The appearance of this pretty square, however, is dominated by the baroque parish church, Sant Miquel del Port. The church is flanked by a house in which Ferdinand de Lesseps, the builder of the Suez Canal, lived during his time as French Consul in Barcelona.

All the streets in Barceloneta lead to the beach, including Carrer Almirall Cervera with its many fish restaurants. One rather inconspicuous feature is a fountain dedicated to flamenco dancer Carmen Amaya who grew up in Barcelona. The designer beach promenade, Passeig Marítim has replaced the old, picturesque beach bars and restaurants, with their chairs set up on the sand. Now they have been moved on. Some have new premises in the transformed Port Vell complex, others in the Olympic Port area. Barceloneta's beach, Platja San Salvador, is the first of five distinct strands separated by breakwaters, which now make up the city's leisure seafront. They are a vast improvement on the delapidated shore that straggled alongside this former industrial area, and the sea, prey

The beach on Passeig Marítim

to sewage, shipping and refinery detritus, has also been considerably cleaned up.

At the northern end of Passeig Marítim is a viewing tower. From here there is an excellent view over the neighbouring **Vila Olímpica**. Today, modern architecture rises up into the heavens. Yet just a few years ago, this area was one of the bleakest in the city, and certainly would not have attracted tourists. Disused industrial sites and scrap yards could be found here, along with slums which housed the poorest of the poor.

Vila Olímpica

The 1992 Olympic Games offered a welcome opportunity to clear up the area. A tasteful marina was developed, which served as the starting point for the Olympic regattas. The Olympic village complex, overlooked by a pair of towers (one of which is a hotel) has become a new symbol of the city. Some 2,000 flats were for sale here, and they went like hot cakes, even though the owners couldn't move in until the games were over. This new district is called Nova Icària and connects with the Barceloneta beaches to make a 6-km (4-mile) long beach promenade, including a hospital which was used to treat the athletes during the games.

39

The bustling restaurants which line the Olympic Port have become a popular place to eat at weekends and every night of the week. It is hard to imagine any city that offers so much choice of food in such a small space. Even Planet Hollywood is here, at the base of Frank Gehry's giant fish which dominates the port area. Recommended restaurants in Barceloneta include: Aitor, an excellent four-star restaurant, Carrer Carbonell 5; Antigua Casa Solé is for fish lovers and has a rustic atmosphere, Carrer Sant Carles; Can Tipa has simple and reasonably priced dishes, cooked in fisherman's style, Passeig Joan de Borbó 6.

Eating out at night

Montjuïc

Allow at least half a day for this route around the 200-m (660-ft) high Montjuïc to the south of the old city. To take in the interesting museums on the hill as well, a full day is necessary. Montjuïc can be reached by car from the port by going down Passeig Josep Carner and then along Carretera de Miramar. Alternatively, starting from Plaça d'Espanya go along Reina Maria Cristina and then Marquès de Comillas. If you don't have a car you can either use the funicular which goes from the metro station Paral.lel almost to the top of the hill, or go by foot following the route described below. This starts at Plaça d'Espanya and goes up through the parks.

The unusual name for this strategically important raised area, where the Romans built a temple complex, comes either from the Latin *Mons jovis* (Mountain of Jupiter), or from *Montjueu* (the Jewish Mountain). In the Middle Ages there was a Jewish cemetery here. In 1929 the hill was chosen as the site of Barcelona's second Universal Exposition, and impressive gardens and buildings were created.

Standing at the **Plaça d'Espanya**, the most obvious features are the two tower-like obelisks by the architect Reventós, which are modelled on the San Marco tower in Venice. From here you have the best view of the grand flight of steps (today complete with escalator on the side), which leads up to the Palau Nacional (*see below*). Go through the former entrance to the Universal Exposition and various exhibition halls can be seen to the left and right of the Avinguda de la Reina Maria Cristina. Trade fairs are held here all year round. The bull-fighting arena on the

40

The obelisks at Plaça d'Espanya

Bullfighting arena

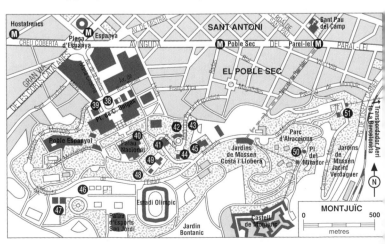

Steps in Plaça d'Espanya

north side of the Plaça d'Espanya is no longer used, and there are plans to use this too for fairs and exhibitions.

You will soon come to the Plaça Carles Buïgas, named after the man who built the fountain which dominates the square. This is the ★★ **Font Màgica** ㊳. This 'magic fountain' spurts its water up into the air every evening in summer in front of the illuminated **Palau Nacional** (9pm–midnight). On Saturday and Sunday there is even musical accompaniment between 10–11pm. The most impressive day is 23 June, when the hill is lit up by the fireworks of the Sant Joan Festival. Controlled by computers, fountains consisting of more than 3,000 jets spray water in hundreds of different colours.

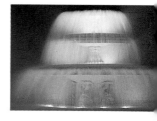

The Font Màgica

Turn right into the Avinguda del Marquès de Comillas, which zig-zags its way up the hill. Immediately on the left is a building which only reappeared here in 1986, the ★ **Pavelló Mies van der Rohe** ㊴. Built on this site for the Universal Exposition in 1929, it was taken down at the end of the event, then faithfully replicated 57 years later on the initiative of a group of Catalan artists. This work, by the architect Mies van der Rohe (1886–1969), was Germany's contribution to the Universal Exposition, and is a classic example of the Bauhaus style. In stark contrast to modernism, its lines display clear right angles. It has flat surfaces of marble and glass, without any decoration or colouring, and open-plan rooms which flow into each other and are situated around a pool. All these features contribute to the cool and subtle appearance of the pavilion, making it a notable exception to the many attractive but somewhat overdone constructions on Montjuïc.

Mies van der Rohe also designed his own armchair for the pavilion, from chrome-plated steel with leather upholstery. The *Barcelona Chair* is now regarded as one of the classic examples of modern design and copies are still produced today.

The Barcelona Chair

Following the Avinguda further up the hill leads to the ★★ **Poble Espanyol**. This 'Spanish village' – an interesting pot-pourri of replicas of buildings from different Spanish regions – was the way Spain presented itself to visitors at the Universal Exposition in 1929. The entrance to this collection of construction styles is through the Puerta de San Vicente, part of the city wall from Ávila in Castile. Among other items on display are buildings from Aragón at the Plaça Aragonesa, an Andalusian quarter (Barri Andaluz) and, in the Calle del Principe, palaces and houses from the Basque provinces.

Although uninhabited, the village is a distinctly lively open-air museum, popular with the locals, containing a wealth of bars, restaurants, artisan workshops and craft shops. There is even a glass factory where production can be observed. In the evening the Plaça Major, the market square, becomes a fairground. Music comes from every direction, particularly from the El Tablao de Carmen restaurant, a magnet for visitors, where typical Andalusian food is accompanied by tourist-style flamenco from 9pm until dawn. A double decker bus runs free of charge every half an hour from Plaça d'Espanya to the Poble Espanyol.

Behind the Spanish village runs the Avinguda dels Montanyans, which leads eastwards directly to the Palau Nacional. This monumental but rather kitschy building was due to have been pulled down in 1934 but was recently rebuilt to become one of the most important museums in the city, the ★★★ **Museu d'Art de Catalunya** (MNAC) **⓵**. It has acquired a world-wide reputation through its unique collection of Romanesque frescos and sculptures, along with its Gothic works. Around AD1000, wonderful wall paintings were created in Catalonia, particularly in the remote valleys of the Pyrenees. Most of them portrayed biblical scenes. Amongst other great works the museum contains the apse from the Santa Maria de Taüll church with its scene of David and Goliath. The delightful *Pantocrátor* (Christ as the ruler of the world, 1123) from Sant Climent de Taüll is an absolute masterpiece of the Taüll school. There are also apses from the area around Seu d'Urgell, holy figures and altarpieces. Nearly half of the museum is devoted to Romanesque art.

Museu d'Art de Catalunya

The Gothic section includes retables and paintings by Joan Rexach (*Sant Ursula*, 1468), Lluís Dalmau (*Virgen de Consellers*, 1445) and Catalan painter Jaume Huguet (1415–1495, *see pages 28* and *31*). Renaissance and baroque art, as well as that from later periods, are represented by such renowned artists as Francisco de Ribalta, José de Ribera (*The Martyrdom of Saint Bartholomew, 1644*), Velázquez (*Saint Paul*, c 1619) and El Greco. (Daily except Tuesday 9am–9pm.)

From the Palau Nacional the way leads up Passeig de Santa Madrona to the **Museu Etnològic** ❹.The Ethnological Museum is also located in a building which was constructed for the Universal Exposition of 1929, and presents cultural exhibits from all around the world. Of particular interest is the Latin American section. (Monday 3–8.30pm, Tuesday to Friday 9am–8.30pm, Sunday 9am–2pm.)

Museu Etnològic

On the same street is another museum occupying one of the 1929 Exposition buildings, the **Museu Arqueològic** ❹. It contains collections of prehistoric, Iberian, Phoenician, Carthaginian, Greek, Roman and Visigothic art. Particularly outstanding are the findings from the Greek settlement Empòrion near L'Escala on the Costa Brava, including the famous statue of the God Asklepios. (Tuesday to Saturday 9.30am–1.00pm and 4–7pm, Sunday 9am–2pm.)

Museu Arqueològic

From the archaeological museum the route continues further up through the Jardins de Laribal. This is one of many gardens on Montjuïc and is famous for its roses. On the edge of the gardens is the **Teatre Grec** ❹. This amphitheatre (1929) has excellent acoustics, with rows of seats built into the hill in classic Greek style. Concerts and theatre performances take place here in July and August, during the *Festival Grec*.

The open-air Teatre Grec

Continuing along the Passeig de Santa Madrona in the direction of the Olympic stadium, brings you to the **Font del Gat** ❹ restaurant on the left. This has very romantic grounds which were originally an old estate. From the theatre, steps lead up to the buildings of the ★★ **Fundació Joan Miró** ❹. Miró (1893–1983) was born in Barcelona and created a variety of works in his home town, even though he spent much of his life in Tarragona and Mallorca. Amongst his works are the *Dona i Ocell* (Woman with Bird) sculpture in the Miró Park (*see page 57*), ceramic walls at the airport and the floor mosaics at Plaça de Boqueria in the Ramblas (*see page 19*). Miró set up the foundation himself in 1971 with his friend Joan Prats. The museum and a study centre were opened in 1975 and extended in 1986. The plans were by the Catalan architect Josep Lluís Sert. More than 150 paintings, sculptures and over 5,000 drawings are on display in the airy rooms of the museum, covering each of the surrealist's creative periods. Works from Miró's contemporaries can also be seen, whilst numerous special exhibitions are devoted to up-and-coming artists. The spacious rooms and grounds are also increasingly being used for a wide variety of cultural events, including cabaret and children's theatre. (Tuesday to Saturday 11am–7pm, Sunday 10.30am–2.30pm.) In the inner courtyard there is a lovely restaurant where you can relax and have a snack.

From the Fundació Miró

Part of the Olympic complex

In the Jardins de Joan Maragall

The foundation itself is at Plaça Neptù. From here it is worth making a short detour up Avinguda de L'Estadi to the ★ **Olympic Stadium**. The main facade of the stadium (Estadi Olímpic) dates back to 1929, whilst the stands and the technical facilities are new and meet all the needs of a modern sports arena. Only the limited capacity, with space for 'just' 50,000 spectators, caused problems at the 1992 Olympic Games, since the large opening and closing ceremonies took place here. Other important venues in the so-called Olympic Ring (Anella Olímpica) on Montjuïc were: the Palau Sant Jordi, designed by Arata Isozaki, which with 17,000 seats is one of the largest (and most striking) sports halls in the world; the Olympic swimming stadium, Bernat Picornell ㊻, from 1970, which was renovated and enlarged for the games; and the hall of the INEFC sports school ㊼ (judo and wrestling) with 6,000 seats. Athletics, riding and ball sports events all took place on Montjuïc, along with a number of the swimming events.

Around the Olympic stadium are interesting ★ **gardens**. Below the stadium are the botanical gardens, **Jardins de Joan Maragall** ㊽, now nearly 100 years old. The **Palau Albéniz** ㊾ is situated in this venerable plant paradise. This small palace, named after the famous composer, is now used as the King's official residence when in Barcelona. It can be visited on Sundays (10am–2pm) if not in use. On the southern slope of Montjuïc is the Jardí Botànic, laid out with terraces, and including a herbarium, an observation tower, a library and a research laboratory.

From the Olympic stadium head back to the Fundació and on to the Plaça Dante. Here is the Miramar station for the funicular railway to the metro station Paral.lel, and a small restaurant. From here you can either take a cable car up to the Castell de Montjuïc or go by foot. On the way you will pass the Jardins de Mossèn Jacint Verdaguer (on the right), named after a famous Catalan author (1845–1902), and the Parc d'Atraccions (1931), the second most important amusement park in the city, after the children's paradise on Tibidabo (*see page 60*). In the Parc d'Atraccions there is everything that could possibly delight the hearts of the young (and the not so young), including carousels, kiosks and sweets. (Open daily 4.30–10.15pm; Saturday and Sunday from noon.)

Riding the cable car

The fortress ★ **Castell de Montjuïc** (from 1640) does not exactly arouse good memories in the Barcelonans. At the beginning of the 18th century the Bourbon king Philip V used it to incarcerate numerous Catalans after he took control of the city (*see Historical Highlights*). Later, during the civil war, many republicans were imprisoned in the fortress, which today houses a military museum. (Tuesday to Saturday 10am–noon and 4–7.30pm, Sunday 10am–7.30pm.) From the fortress, with its terrifying cannons, there is a wonderful view over the city of Barcelona and the waterfront.

Continue uphill along the Carretera de Montjuïc, past the **Sardana memorial** 🄳 (for a description of the sardana, the Catalan national dance, *see page 81*) by Catalan artist Josep Canyas, and you come to a viewing point, the **Mirador de L'Alcalde** 🄴, with a fantastic view over the port. Once again there is the choice of going on by foot or taking a cable car. Numerous paths lead through the Jardins de Mossèn Costa i Llobera with its sub-tropical plants which thrive splendidly on the wind-protected southeast slopes of Montjuïc.

The Sardana memorial

Those with a sense of adventure (and who do not suffer from vertigo) can take the cable car system that crosses the entire 1.3-km (¾-mile) length of the port area, at a height of 100m (330ft), before arriving in the Barceloneta district. The ★ **Transbordador Aéri** is supported by two towers, which dominate the appearance of the port: Jaume I (107m/350ft) and Sant Sebastià (85m/280ft). The cable cars are only in operation when the weather is good, and in particular when it is not too windy. (Tuesday to Sunday approximately noon–8pm.)

The Transbordador Aéri

A good way to complete this route is with a stroll along the beach at Barceloneta (*see page 38*) and with a bite to eat, for example in one of the fish restaurants on the Passeig Joan de Borbó. Here you will be served with reasonably priced – and freshly caught – seafood delicacies with *pa amb tomàquet* (*see page 84*). To return to Barcelona take the metro from the Barceloneta station or a bus from the Passeig Joan de Borbó.

Route 5

Passeig de Gràcia – Temple de la Sagrada Família

A good half day is needed (including the visits) for the walk along the Passeig de Gràcia and the Carrer de Provença to the Templo de la Sagrada Família and, if you have the energy, on to the Hospital de Sant Pau.

Passeig de Gràcia

The route begins at the Plaça de Catalunya (*see page 16*) and heads northwest along the ★ **Passeig de Gràcia**, a magnificent boulevard 60m (200ft) wide and 1.2km (¾ mile) long. Until the beginning of the 19th century, however, it was a barely made-up country road, joining the city with the village of Gràcia. In 1827 five lanes were built and in 1861 there was regular coach traffic and later a horse-drawn tram. Passeig de Gràcia reached its peak around the turn of the century, when it became the main axis for the futuristic construction concepts of architect Ildefons Cerdà (*see page 75*). A royal decree of 1859 gave him the job of solving the city's housing shortage by building a completely new district, the Eixample (literally, expansion). As a result the dusty country road became the focal point of a residential area for the rich bourgeoisie and, particularly in the 20th century, acquired a snobbish and money-centred image. The first constructions in the new district around the Passeig were residential buildings with just two or three floors. Gradually, however, the buildings became taller and posh businesses, banks and insurance companies moved in.

Casa Pons i Pasqual

A good example is the first house on the right hand side (Nos 2–4), the **Casa Pons i Pasqual** ❷, designed by Enric Sagnier i Villavecchia (1858–1931). This delightful house, with its black towers, became the high-class address of a bank, an insurance company, a travel office and then a fast-food restaurant. The next houses, the **Cases Antoni Rocamora** ❸ (No 6–14, architect Joaquim Bassegoda i Amigó, 1854–1938) are owned by a long-established clothing business. Diagonally opposite, on the corner of Gran Via de les Corts Catalanes, is a particularly eye-catching classical building from 1864 (**No 21**). With its mighty dome and a mythical creature on top, it towers over all the other buildings.

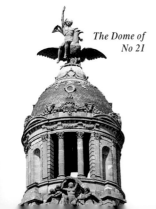

The Dome of No 21

Staying on the left-hand side of the street, the route leads past house No 27, the **Casa Manuel Margarida** ❹ (architect, Joaquim Condina i Matalí, died 1910) to the corner of Passeig de Gràcia and Consell de Cent. Here a unique collection of buildings begins, bringing together superb examples of the most varied architectural styles in one place. As a result the locals call it – half lovingly, half cynically – ★★ **Mansana de la Discòrdia** – The Block of Discord.

Situated directly on the corner is the first house, the **Casa Lleó Morera** (No 35). This house was built in 1905 and designed by Domènech i Montaner (*see page 78*). Even from the outside his trademark can clearly be recognised, with the mirror-like arrangement of the architectural elements around a main axis, crowned by a filigree dome. The smooth outer wall is broken up by window fronts which are richly decorated with columns.

Casa Lleó Morera

Domènech was a master of well-balanced designs, without making his compositions over elaborate. Inside he give his fantasy considerably more leeway than on the facade. Every detail has been individually designed. There are a variety of door handles, coloured ceilings, wooden inlays, and ceramics, all bearing witness to his enormous, impulsive creativity. The centre for the Ruta del Modernisme (*see page 75*) is located in this building. Even if you don't have time to follow the whole route, this house may be visited individually, and is well worth it. For details, tel: 93 488 0139.

The next house along (No 37) is the **Casa Ramon Mulleras** (1904). This building by Enric Sagnier i Villavecchia (1858–1931) – who designed many houses in the so-called Golden Quadrangle (Quadrat d'Or) of Eixample – is perhaps the least eye-catching of the Block of Discord. The only unusual features are the bays with arches and double columns. Otherwise the building is trapped in the rather conservative neo-Gothic style of the turn of the century.

Casa Ramon Mulleras

House No 39 leads you by the nose into a paradise: Egyptian and rococo scents and the favourite aromas of kings and queens caress the olfactory senses in the **Museu del Perfum**. The bottles and other scent containers also reflect the fashions of past epochs. (Monday to Friday 10.30am–1pm and 5–7.30pm.)

MUSEU
DEL
PERFUM

At No 41 is the **Casa Amatller**. Constructed in 1900, this building shows the preference of Puig i Cadafalch for mixing elements from different styles. There are bays decorated in Gothic style, wrought-iron balconies of Italian appearance, and a tiled front in best Catalan style. And the whole edifice is crowned by a Flemish stepped gable. Inside is an entrance hall with columns, designed like a courtyard, and a stairway with a splendid stained-glass dome. Cadafalch was perhaps the most intellectual of the three greats of modernism (*see page 75*), and the least cautious in terms of external effects. Apart from the entrance hall, the house cannot be visited.

Doorway, Casa Batlló

★★ **Casa Batlló**, is at No 43. Gaudí's houses often explain stories, and this one is no exception. The cross of Saint George is stuck into the dragon's back on the tiled ceramic roof. Under its body the dragon has collected the bones (the balconies) and skeletons (the bays on the ground floor) of its victims. Gaudí shows his preference for natural forms here. Everything is round and flowing. Only the windows on the upper floors are square, although the balconies give them the appearance of staring eyes. The outer wall – a mosaic of ceramic pieces – radiates a Mediterranean colourfulness. Gaudí was also responsible for the interior design of this 'mystical' house. The Casa Batlló shows quite clearly that the great architect was an impulsive, almost fanatical artist in terms of the way he worked with many materials. Visits can only be made as part of the Ruta del Modernismo (*see page 75*).

Go on to the Carrer Aragó and turn left. After a few metres you will see an astonishing building (No 255). Above an art nouveau facade sits a tangle of sculpted wire. This former publishing house, Montaner i Simón, was built by Domènech i Montaner between 1881 and 1886. Since 1990 it has housed the ★ **Fundació Antoni Tàpies** (Tuesday to Sunday, 11am–8pm). This foundation was set up in

Windows, Casa Batlló

1984 by the artist himself (born 1923) with the object of promoting modern art and culture. On the upper floor is the private library of the artist and sculptor, and in the entrance area a small shop sells books about him and his works. The works themselves hang in the hall of the former printers. Exhibitions of works by other artists are shown in the cellar.

Opinions differ widely on Tàpies, whose *Informel* style of art works with abstract forms, mythical symbols and formulas. Some regard him as a talented storyteller, who is able to express the feelings of strange worlds through simple forms such as the cross, numbers and letters of the alphabet. Others regard this self-educated artist as being simply abstract, speaking in puzzles without any impulsive power.

Undisputed, however, is Tàpies' creativity with new techniques. Through his use of oil, sand, rubbed marble and varnish he achieves a three-dimensional collage on his enormous canvasses. He has worked with wood, junk and corroded copper. Symbolic formulas appear in ever-new variations. To Tàpies, painting is an act of meditation, in which he puts himself under creative pressure through the use of materials which harden quickly. The basis for his work, according to his own statements, is his predilection for Eastern philosophy and the deep feeling which the countless walls of his home town, Barcelona, left on him: slogans from the civil war, bullet holes, cracks and graffiti. All have now been ravaged by the passage of time and yet at the same time acquired greater poignancy. In Barcelona Tàpies is a controversial but revered artist, who also has an excellent reputation abroad.

From the Fundació go back to the Passeig de Gràcia, and head further west on the right-hand side. Go past the **Casa Marfà** ⑤⑤ (No 66, architect Manuel Comas i Thos, born 1855) on the corner of Carrer València, and you will see, on Passeig de Gràcia, the refurbished Majestic hotel. Whatever the weather, a liveried page-boy stands in front of the hotel, waiting to meet the magnificent limousines of arriving guests. Go past the **Casa Joan Coma** ⑤⑥ (No 74, architect Enric Sagnier i Villavecchia), and on the corner of Carrer de Provença is the most imposing building of the whole street, the ★★ **Casa Milà** (No 92).

This enormous apartment house was built by Gaudí between 1906 and 1910, and soon acquired the nickname *La Pedrera* (The Pile of Stones). Even amongst the company of other strange buildings, the massive structure appears to be out of place. There is the wave-like form of the roof with its ventilation holes mutated into the shapes of giants and mythical creatures; the concrete and iron construction with no retaining walls; two different inner courtyards, one round, the other elliptical; and the many iron-barred

Tàpies' work on display

Casa Marfà

Casa Milà

La Pedrera's courtyard and stairway

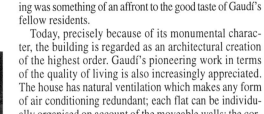

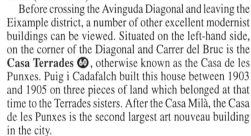

Casa Thomas
In the Palau de Montaner

balconies in front of round windows. All in all the building was something of an affront to the good taste of Gaudí's fellow residents.

Today, precisely because of its monumental character, the building is regarded as an architectural creation of the highest order. Gaudí's pioneering work in terms of the quality of living is also increasingly appreciated. The house has natural ventilation which makes any form of air conditioning redundant; each flat can be individually organised on account of the moveable walls; the corridors all have natural light, and there is even an underground garage in the cellar. Indeed, many of the rented flats from the 1980s fail to reach standards set by this house. Conducted tours (in various languages) through the inner courtyards, stairways and roof take place every day and some evenings. Tel: 93 484 5995.

Turn into the Carrer de Provença near the Casa Milà and head eastwards past three interesting houses: the **Casa Josep Ferrer-Vidal** 57 by Enric Sagnier i Villavecchia (No 267, on the left); the **Casa Pilar Bassols** 58 by Gabriel Borrell i Cardona (No 301, on the left); and, opposite, the **Cases Francesc Lalanne** 59 by Arnau Calvet i Peyronill (1875–1956).

Before crossing the Avinguda Diagonal and leaving the Eixample district, a number of other excellent modernist buildings can be viewed. Situated on the left-hand side, on the corner of the Diagonal and Carrer del Bruc is the **Casa Terrades** 60, otherwise known as the Casa de les Punxes. Puig i Cadafalch built this house between 1903 and 1905 on three pieces of land which belonged at that time to the Terrades sisters. After the Casa Milà, the Casa de les Punxes is the second largest art nouveau building in the city.

Turning right into the Carrer Bruc and then right into the Carrer de Mallorca brings you to the **Casa Thomas** 61 (No 291–293). This impressive building by Domènech i Montaner was built between 1895 and 1898. Nowadays the furnishing house B D Ediciones uses the ground floor to display its wares, including replicas of Gaudí's furniture. Originally the house had just two floors. The balconies and the towers were added later. At the junction of Carrer Roger de Llúria is the Pompeiian-styled **Palau Casades** 62 on the right. On the left is the **Palau de Montaner** 63, also by Domènech i Montaner, which today is the seat of the representatives of the Madrid government.

Now go back down the Carrer de Provença towards the Diagonal and cross over the Passeig de Sant Joan. A little way up to the left, on the right hand side, is the **Casa Macaya** 64 (No 108). This art nouveau house was built by Puig i Cadafalch in 1901 and is today used to house regular exhibitions by the cultural section of the 'la Caixa' (a major Catalan savings bank). The stairwell has an extraordinary flower design in the wall plaster.

Further up the Carrer Mallorca, the Plaça de la Sagrada Família is only a few minutes away. In the middle of a park area, with a lake and a children's playground, is Barcelona's most famous symbol, the ★★★ **Temple de la Sagrada Família**.

Sagrada Família

The Casa Milà (1910) was Gaudí's last secular construction. From then on until his death in 1926 he devoted himself to the completion of his life's work, the 'Temple of the Holy Family'. Yet he never experienced the completion of his 'basilica for the poor' as he called it. Indeed it could be a few generations more before it is finally finished.

Gaudí took over the responsibility for the basilica in 1883. The previous architect, Francisco del Villar, had an argument with the authorities and left the project. Originally the Sagrada Família was supposed to be a traditional, neo-Gothic church, and despite having his own ideas, Gaudí had to accept the ground plan which was already there. He completed the crypt – where his own somewhat neglected tomb can be seen today – following Villar's classical style. Then he set out on the realisation of his gigantic plans for the overground part: a basilica with 18 towers, 12 for the apostles, four for the evangelists, one for Mary, and the highest as a symbol of Christ, rising up 170m (560ft) into the sky. The church was planned to measure 110m (360ft) by 45m (150ft) with room for 15,000 of the faithful inside. For the eastern portal Gaudí took the birth of Jesus as his theme, for the western portal Christ's suffering, and for the main portal Christ as the glorious ruler of the world. Gaudí only managed to complete one of the 105-m (340-ft) high towers over the eastern portal – the tower dedicated to Saint Barnabus (Bernabeu). The rest of the eastern portal was completed

Sagrada Família: recent additions to the western portal

after Gaudí's death, in the period up to 1935, by one of his colleagues, Sugrañes.

The incredible amount of work which went into this magnificent creation can only really be appreciated with binoculars: faith, love and hope are chiselled into the stone of the three entrances of the portal. Rampant plant decorations, numerous animal figures (one portal is supported by tortoises, the other by turtles), and the path of the stars through the year are joined together in flowing compositions. Among other figures, Christ's family tree, the crib with the shepherds and the three kings, the flight to Egypt, and the young Jesus in the temple can all be recognised.

Christ's family tree

However, portrayals of realistic figures were not amongst Gaudí's strengths. Here they seem a little out of place, as if consciously to conceal the genius of the tower constructions, which continue up from their rectangular bases in circular form. Gaudí left behind detailed plans for the construction of the western facade, but they were only partly followed when building continued after 1952. For many people the portal front, with its massive sculptures by Josep María Subirachs, is a bone of contention. It was finished after 1976 with the help of donations, but for many Barcelonans it is too static and too modern, and fails to fit into the overall character of what Gaudí intended to be the 'basilica of the 20th century'. As a result, there are a number of voices calling for the church to be left in its present condition, as a memorial to the greatest modernist architect.

52

Tower pinnacle

The towers of the eastern facade can be climbed on foot (for those who do not suffer from vertigo) or ascended in a lift. The reward is a wonderful view over the city. A delightful little museum has been set up under the basilica with the architect's plans, models (including the church in Santa Coloma de Cervello, where Gaudí acquired the experience for the Sagrada Família, *see page 73*) and various of Gaudí's personal effects. Opening times for the church and museum: Monday to Saturday 9am–8pm. Also open on Sunday in the high season.

Facade of the hospital

The Avinguda de Gaudí – newly designed by the architect Quintana, with wrought-iron lanterns and sculptures – leads from Gaudí's masterpiece to a work of his modernist colleague Domènech i Montaner, the **Hospital de la Santa Creu i de Sant Pau ㊹**. This present day university clinic was built between 1902 and 1912 and deliberately avoids a clinical atmosphere. Spacious gardens surround a row of pavilions, which are connected together underground. The slim tower, with its Moorish influenced art nouveau decoration, radiates joy and harmony. The intention of the architect was to create a soothing, humane atmosphere for the patients in order to distract them from their suffering.

Route 6

Reial Monestir de Pedralbes

Pedralbes and the surrounding area

There are all sorts of interesting sights beyond the city centre, including traces of Roman remains, art nouveau and
contemporary culture in the tranquil Pedralbes area. It is
also possible to combine the journey here with a visit to
the Sarrià district, or the university area in the Les Corts
district. Near the university is the giant football stadium
of what is probably Spain's most famous club, FC
Barcelona (Barça). Allow a good half day for the tour,
as it involves a longish trip on the city railway (FGC).

Start at the Plaça de Catalunya, and take the FGC to
Reina Elisenda. After a 10-minute walk southeast along
Passeig de Reina Elisenda Montcada and Carrer del Bisbe
Català, you will see a monastery building on the right-hand
side, the ★★ **Reial Monestir de Pedralbes**. From the outside the most striking feature of this singled-aisled Gothic
church, dating from 1419, is the facade. Inside is the **tomb**
of the monastery's founder, Queen Elisenda, who spent
the last 30 years of her life here, after her husband, Jaume
II, died. Entrance on Sunday between 10am–1pm and on
weekdays for the evening communion at 7.30pm.

Tomb of Elisenda

The **Santa Maria convent** (1327) can be entered
through a side door. Amusingly, at the behest of the queen,
the convent was originally led by six Franciscan monks.
On the left-hand (south) side is the conference room –
which contains a number of sacred objects – and the dormitory, whose sleeping quarters have been preserved in
their original condition. Photography is forbidden. In the
western wing is the refectory with a kitchen, and behind
it is the queen's private palace. Going past the day rooms
in the north wing brings you to the Sant Miquel chapel
in the church wall on the eastern side. The chapel is dec-

Painting in the convent

53

orated with beautiful paintings from around 1345 by the Catalan artist Ferrer Bassa.

The most impressive feature of the monastery complex is undoubtedly the Gothic ★★ **cloister**. It consists of two columned passageways, one above the other. A further, narrower passageway was added on top in the 15th century. In the middle is a Renaissance style fountain. The Thyssen Collection is housed in the nuns' former dormitory and a nearby room. It comprises 72 paintings, mostly of Italian origin, and is part of the famous Thyssen-Bornemisza foundation whose principal exhibition is in the Villahermosa Palace in Madrid.

The route now leads down the hill along the Avinguda de Pedralbes. On both sides of the street there are new luxury apartments, surrounded by extensive green areas, a stark contrast to the old part of the city. Like neighbouring Sarrià to the northeast, Pedralbes is a residential area for the upper income groups. After about 15 minutes, turn off to the left into Carrer Bosch i Gimpera. This leads to the main sights of the **Sarrià** district, which was incorporated into Barcelona in the middle of the 19th century. Among the points of interest are the **Capuchin monastery** in the Carrer del Cardinal Vives, the main shopping street, Carrer Mayor de Sarrià and, turning off this street into Carrer de Cornet i Mas, the 14th-century parish church of Sant Vicenç.

54

Facade of the Capuchin monastery

Bordering on the Carrer Bosch i Gimpera are the grounds of the Reial Club de Tennis, the Royal Tennis Club, where the ATP tournament is held every year.

Going further down the Avinguda de Pedralbes leads shortly to the colourful buildings of the **Finca Güell**. The artistic wrought-iron ★ **entrance gate**, representing a dragon with two wings, immediately grabs the attention. The dragon used to raise its claws in threatening manner when the gate was opened, and guarded over the country residence of the wealthy Güell family, whose grounds stretched as far as the other side of the Avinguda Diagonal (to the Les Corts district). Gaudí built the portal complex for the Güell family between 1884 and 1887, with a 10-m (33-ft) high tower, and a porter's house with a copper roof. Near a large mansion (today the Palau Reial de Pedralbes, *see next page*) there are various pavilions which once served as stables. The buildings are made of red brick, and some of the decorations are reminiscent of Moorish style. The colourful appearance of the pavilions (mainly blue and white) comes from the typical Gaudí ceramic mosaics. The Güell Pavilions are not open to visitors, however; they are now home to the Càtedra Gaudí and a department of the architectural college.

Entrance gate, Finca Güell

A few metres away from the pavilions, but still in the grounds of the former Güell estate, is the **Parc de Pe-**

dralbes where students from the nearby university come to relax between lectures.

At the northern end of the park is the **Palau Reial de Pedralbes**. The palace was a present from the city to King Alfonso XIII, and was constructed between 1919 and 1924 by rebuilding and extending the Güells' former stately house. Unfortunately, in the process a number of Gaudí's works were removed from the palace, including a richly decorated fireplace. The reason for building the palace was that there had previously been no suitable premises for royal functions in Barcelona. Later Franco also used the building. Today the yellow coloured building – which is decorated with wall paintings, and whose grounds include a large pool with **statues** – houses the ★★**Museu Ceràmica**. The artistic use of ceramics has a long tradition in Catalonia, as evidenced by the beautiful tiled ceramic facades on many buildings in the city, or Gaudí's oft-used *trencadís* technique of putting together small pieces of ceramic. In Martorell (*see page 72*) there are two large museums, the L'Enrajolada and the Vincenç Ros, which document the history of Catalan ceramic art. The Palau museum exhibits objects from the 8th century onwards in 15 rooms spread over two floors. Its focus, however, is on contemporary works. Ceramic creations by Miró, Picasso and others are displayed to good advantage in the stylish palace. (Tuesday to Friday 9am–2pm, Saturday and Sunday 10am–1pm.)

Statue in the Palau Reial grounds

MUSEU DE CERÀMICA

55

Crossing over the Avinguda Diagonal we come to the **Zona Universitària**, where the 'new university' was built after World War II, when the premises of the 'old university' around Plaça Universitat became too small.

South of the Ciutat Universitària, but also in the Les Corts district, is the FC Barcelona football club. The club has a rich tradition and is often affectionately simply called 'Barça'. The home of the club which so often has been Spanish champion is the **Camp Nou Stadium**, which was built in 1957 and extended in 1987. With room for 120,000 spectators it is one of the largest stadiums in the world. Watching the local team play against arch-rivals Real Madrid is an unforgettable experience, with an atmosphere more like a festival. Also here is the club's football museum, containing cups, trophies, pennants, photos, and videos from the the sports club's history. A visit to the museum includes a view over the huge round stadium from the president's box. The club was formed in 1899 and also has a famous basketball team. Opening times for the museum: Tuesday to Friday 10am–1pm and 4–6pm, Saturday and Sunday 10am–1pm.

To get back to the city centre either go the Collblanc metro station to the south of the stadium or the Palau Reial stop to the north.

Camp Nou Stadium

Additional Sights

City centre

Museu d'Història de la Medicina de Catalunya. Passatge Mercader 11, FGC station Provença. **M** Passeig de Gràcia, Diagonal, tel: 93 216 0500. More than 2,500 exhibits in 14 rooms document the history of Catalan medicine. They include medical instruments from the 19th century and the personal belongings of famous doctors. Open Thursday 10am–1pm, or ring to arrange a time.

Museu de la Música

Museu de la Música. Avinguda Diagonal 373. **M** Diagonal. Precious instruments and interesting documents from the history of music fill the rooms of the Casa Quadras. This former residence of Count Quadras was modernised – both inside and outside – in 1904 by Puig i Cadafalch (*see page 79*). Behind the heavy iron portal is a fantastic variety of types of decoration: neo-Gothic, plateresque and floral decorations cover the walls and ceiling like carpets. The museum, spread over three floors, contains an exquisite collection of pianos, organs, wind and percussion instruments as well as fine string instruments. After all, Spanish guitar makers such as the Andalusian Ramírez have world-wide reputations. Soon to be re-housed in the new Auditorium (Plaça de les Glòries). Open Tuesday to Sunday, 9am–2pm.

56

★★**Palau de la Música Catalana** ㊲. Carrer Sant Francesc de Paula 2. **M** Urquinaona, tel: 93 268 1000 for tickets or tours. Dating from 1908, this impressive concert hall stands on the edge of the working-class Sant Pere district, not far from the Via Laietana. The architect Domènech i Montaner was contracted to build the palace

Palau de la Música Catalana

by the *Orfeó Català* choir club, which was founded in 1891. One of the streets where the building stands is named after the co-founder of the choir, Amadeus Vives. The other founder was Luís Millet.

The outside of the red-brick building is impressive, and in recent years the appearance has been improved further by the addition of a new side entrance. On the southeast corner is an exceptional sculpture, *La Cançó Popular Catalana* by Miquel Blay, portraying singers who are ordinary people from all walks of life. Over the main entrance are busts of famous composers, including Bach, Beethoven, Wagner and Palestrina. The splendour of the inside is overwhelming: the audience sits beneath a colourful, bead-shaped stained glass ceiling, surrounded by sculptures (including Beethoven and Valkyries on horseback), beautiful lamps and ceramic floral ornaments. Most of these are the work of the sculptors Arnau and Gargallo, who worked together with Domènech i Montaner. One could easily be distracted from the music by the impressive surroundings.

Although acoustic considerations played no role in the overall design of the concert hall, and the stage had to be extended a few years ago, the sound quality in this music palace is actually excellent. This is the home of the state orchestra, although jazz and pop concerts are also held here. Ticket sales from 10am–9pm, Monday to Saturday.

Parc de l'Espanya Industrial

Parc de l'Espanya Industrial. Carrer de Muntades. **M** Tarragona. This post-modernist park is a symbol of the *Nou Urbanisme* concept of city architecture. The idea is to make modern art an integral part of the cityscape, particularly in recreational areas. The park is right next to the main railway station, Central-Sants. Seat terraces were built around an artificial lake, in accordance with the plans of Basque architect Luis Peña Canchegui. These terraces are separated by 10 huge towers. In contrast to the severe appearance of these constructions, however, are the green areas with sculptures by Manuel Fuxà (*Neptune*), Anthony Caro and Andrés Nagel (*Saint George and the Dragon*). The enormous iron monster by Nagel is particularly popular with children on account of its integrated slide.

Parc Joan Miró. Carrer Tarragona. **M** Plaça d'Espanya. Less than 10 minutes away from the Parc Industrial is another of Barcelona's recreational areas, the Miró Park, also known as L'Escorxador, as this was formerly the site of an abattoir. The park is the same size as four Eixample blocks and unfortunately has all too few trees. On a small island in the middle of a pool is the famous symbol of this park, Miró's gigantic sculpture called *Dona i Ocell* (Woman with Bird).

Dona i Ocell

Plaça de Toros – the bull-fighting museum. Gran Via de les Corts Catalanes 749. **M** Monumental. This arena is immediately recognisable from a distance by the two enormous blue and white tiled eggs over the entrance. Situated on the Gran Via de les Corts Catalanes the arena is also known as 'Monumental'. This is now Barcelona's only flourishing bull-fighting arena, after the second one on the Plaça d'Espanya was closed. There is also a museum, devoted to the *corrida*. On show are the *trajes de luces*, the skin-tight sequinned costumes of the toreadors, along with stuffed bulls, posters, photos and the iron brands of famous bull rearers. Next to the museum is a library and documentation department.

Opening times: during the bull-fighting season, 19 March to 12 October, 10am–1pm and 3.30–7pm; on fight days (usually Wednesday and Sunday) mornings only. Tickets sales: 10.30am–1.10pm and 4–7.30pm at the arena, tel: 93 245 5804, and before the fights. The cheapest tickets are those in the sun (*sol*), medium priced tickets are *sol y sombre* (sun and shade), and the most expensive (*sombre*) are completely covered.

Outlying districts

Museu Clarà. Carrer Calatrava 27–29. FGC station Tres Torres. This museum dedicated to the famous Catalan sculptor Josep Clarà (1878–1957) is in the north of the Sarrià district (*see page 54*). Clarà lived in Paris from 1910 onwards and was heavily influenced by the work of Rodin. His most famous work – *La Deèssa* (The Goddess) – can be admired at the Plaça de Catalunya. In 1969 his former attic rooms were opened to the public as a museum. Open Tuesday to Sunday, 9am–2pm.

Parc del Clot. **M** Clot. Even the north of Barcelona, previously a mainly industrial area, is slowly blossoming. Factory sites – and, in this case, a former marshalling yard – are being turned into green areas with places for children to play. From the brick and iron frames of the old buildings, delicate sheets of water pour down into pools. At night it looks particularly attractive when it is lit by floodlights.

Parc de la Creueta del Coll

Parc de la Creueta del Coll. Passeig de la Mare de Déu. **M** Penitents. This park area, with a lake for swimming and an artificial beach (cleaner and perhaps more inviting than the natural one at Barceloneta), lies to the west of the Parc Güell in the Vallcarca district. On the site of the former quarry of Creueta, it is now a mass of green with wide paths and viewing towers. The park was designed by the architects Josep Martorell and David Mackay, and contains the *Elogi de L'Aigua* (Elegy to Water) sculpture by the Basque artist Eduardo Chillida, which is suspended from steel cables.

Parc del Laberint. Carrer Germans Desvalls. **M** Montbau, and then 15 minutes' walk. This wonderful garden area lies in the north of the city, in the Horta district, beyond Passeig de la Vall d'Hebron. A mansion stands on the former property of Count Alfarrás. This classic building with neo-Moorish decoration, today houses the School of Restoration, and is surrounded by extensive parkland with dainty statues, small temples and a lake with terraces. The park is an oasis for those seeking relaxation. The main attraction is a maze of cypress hedges (the labyrinth which gives the park its name), which the Count had laid out in 1792. Anyone who gets lost in the maze will be rescued from this green idyll in the evening at the latest when the park keepers come round with their shrill whistles, warning that the park is about to close.

Parc del Laberint

★★ Park Güell. Carrer Olot. **M** Lesseps or **M** Vallcarca, and then 15 minutes' walk to the escalators up Baixada de la Glòria. When Gaudí was commissioned by his patron, the wealthy industrialist Eusebi Güell, to build a garden city he chose the Muntanya Pelada, a hill in the west of the former suburb of Gràcia. What exists today is only a rudiment of the project. Soon after building began it became clear that the planned houses wouldn't sell. Construction was halted when war broke out in 1914 with only two houses built, although Gaudí had already achieved an impressive amount of work in the rest of the park. The central part of the settlement was finished: a market hall over a well, supported by 84 columns, some of which stand diagonally. The hall also has a richly decorated mosaic ceiling. Leading up to the hall is a huge flight of stairs, guarded by an enormous coloured lizard which also acts as an overflow for the reservoir. Over the hall is the market square with a wave-shaped surround. The unconventional beauty of the construction lies in the 'snake bench' which runs around it, with its ceramic mosaic. From the terrace there is a wonderful view over the city. Narrow paths criss-cross over the planned centre of the garden city. The viaducts, which are supported by columns, were supposed to connect the individual houses to each other.

Park Güell mosaic

59

The entrance to the park is flanked by two pavilions, which, in typical Gaudí style, have figure-like chimneys and a patriarchal cross on the roof. Near the entrance is a small house, Gaudí's official home between 1906 and his death 20 years later, although he spent most of the last decade of his life living in a small hut on the site of the Sagrada Família (*see page 51*). This house is now the Museu Gaudí, where the artist's furniture and personal effects are on display. Opening times: museum, daily March to November, 10am–2pm and 4–7pm; park, daily 10am–6pm in winter and till sunset in summer (with a café and souvenir shop).

Lizard and fountain

Gaudí Pavilion

La Rotunda, a former dance temple

Excursion 1

Tibidabo – Sant Cugat del Vallès

Tibidabo is one of the most popular day-trip destinations for the people of Barcelona. Children and grandparents flock there at the weekend, either to visit the fun park at the summit or to have a picnic at one of the many picnic spots on the slopes of the mountain.

Described below is the way there by FGC train and rack railway. Allowing time to visit the science museum too, around half a day is needed. Those who also want to go to Sant Cugat del Vallès will need a car and a few hours more, although the monastery can also be reached by train from Plaça de Catalunya. Most of the walking paths in the Parc de Collserola nature reserve around Tibidabo or around Vallvidrera start from public transport stations.

Starting by car from the Avinguda Diagonal go along Via Augusta, Carrer de Balmes and Avinguda del Tibidabo (around 12km/7½ miles) to the 'magic mountain'. The final approach serpentines its way up to the summit, where, except in summer, there are normally sufficient parking places. To experience everyday Barcelonan life, however, visitors should take public transport. The FGC train goes from Plaça de Catalunya to the Tibidabo stop. From here cross the Plaça J Kennedy and on the right-hand side is the stop for the Tramvia Blau. 'The blue tram' is the last example of its kind in Barcelona and has been creaking its way up the hill since 1890. The tram stop is in front of an interesting house, which was formerly called **La Rotunda** and was a glittering dance temple, complete with bordello. Although the passage of time has taken its toll on the building, its lovely dome-shaped tower and extensive grounds are still impressive.

Tibidabo Tram

Those with time to spare needn't take the tram immediately (departures every 20 minutes) but can go a little way on foot, past the school in the Avinguda del Tibidabo and turn left into the Carrer Roman Macaya. Immediately on the right is the Carrer Teodor Roviralta and the highly recommended La Cupula restaurant, with Catalan cooking, at No 37. The roads leads on to the ★ **Museu de la Ciència**, which is well worth visiting. Built in 1981, it was sponsored by "la Caixa". Standing in the recently re-landscaped grounds is something completely different: a model of a submarine from World War II. Inside the museum, to the left of the entrance, is a planetarium, in which the starry sky is projected onto a dome 10m (33ft) in diameter. At the moment, explanations are only in Spanish and Catalan.

The museum itself is on three floors and covers the worlds of optics, mechanics, physics and electronics. It is a hands-on museum where visitors can operate computers and video cameras and set electric motors in motions – great fun, particularly for the younger ones. Interesting temporary exhibitions are held regularly. Opening times: Tuesday to Sunday 10am–8pm. On the ground floor is a cafeteria.

Catalan cuisine

Museu de la Ciència

61

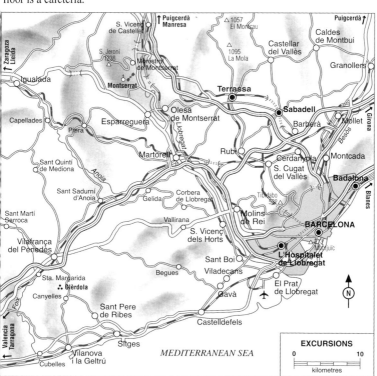

On the way up

Now go back to the tram stop and take the leisurely journey up the mountain to the Estació Inferior. From here a 100-year-old funicular railway brings visitors in a few minutes to the summit of ★★ **Tibidabo** (Plaça Tibidabo station). The view from the top is overwhelming. Below is the sea of houses in the Catalan capital, to the south Montjuïc, to the east the Mediterranean. Although a blanket of smog blocks the view over the city with ever-increasing frequency, on a clear day it is possible to see as far as Mallorca with binoculars. It is also still possible to understand the lovely story of the *Muntanya Màgica*, the 'magic mountain' as the Barcelonans call Tibidabo. Legend has it that on this 532-m (1750-ft) high mountain top, part of the Collserola range, the devil wanted to tempt Jesus with the offer '*Haec omnia tibi dabo si cades adoraberis me*' ('I will give you all this if you worship me'). With these words the devil pointed to the low-lying areas between the Llobregat and Besòs rivers, site of modern-day Barcelona. Hence the name 'Tibidabo'.

Just as the green areas between the rivers have now disappeared, so has the peace on the mountain top. Numerous fast-food restaurants have set up here, and the

Parc d'Atraccions

machinery of the enormous ★ **Parc d'Atraccions** always seems to be in motion. At weekends the park attracts thousands of visitors. From Plaça Tibidabo you go past a number of ticket booths to the terrace-shaped grounds of the park. Here there is every kind of attraction for both young and old: ice-creams, chips, colas, dodgems, big dippers, carousels, a miniature train which goes round the park, a hall of mirrors, a rotating aeroplane from 1928 and much much more. Children will play contentedly here for hours on end. The ★ **Museu d'Autòmates** (Slot Machine Museum) is both amusing and historically interesting. It shows both toys and slot machines from the 19th and early 20th

Mechanical toy

centuries, documenting in the process the transition from the mechanical to the electronic society. Opening times for the amusement park: winter, Saturday, Sunday and public holidays 12–8pm; summer, Monday to Friday 4.30–11pm, Saturday 6.15pm–1am, Sunday and public holidays 12–midnight.

El Sagrat Cor de Jesus

At the highest point of Tibidabo is the **El Sagrat Cor de Jesus** church. This monumental, but kitschy, building was designed by the Sagniers, and is particularly popular for weddings. Enric Sagnier began the project – which was financed by donations – shortly after the turn of the century. But it wasn't until 1952, after the turmoil of the civil war, that the basilica was finished by his son. A neo-Romanesque designed nave with a richly decorated portal forms the base of the church. Above is a neo-Gothic section. The dome of the 67-m (220-ft) high central tower is crowned by a 7.5-m (25-ft) high, 4.8-tonne bronze fig-

ure of Christ, who is looking towards the sea with his arms outstretched. There is a lift to the top of the tower, from where the view is magnificent.

Looking down to the city, one sees on the slope the enormous dome of the Observatori Fabra, which is surrounded by trees. The observatory was founded in 1904 by the astronomer Camilo Fabra and is still in use today.

Pine forests dominate the **Parc de Collserola** nature park, with bushes and scrubs as undergrowth. In some areas strawberries and broom grow, the latter blooming bright yellow in early summer. The variety of birds here is also particularly noticeable, including robins and typical Mediterranean species such as the bee eater. Squirrels and rabbits can also often be seen.

Parc de Collserola

Two kilometres (1¼ miles) to the west of the amusement park is Vallvidrera, in the middle of a park landscape where the remote old villas of the rich Barcelonans are increasingly attracting new neighbours. From here a funicular railway goes down to the FGC station Peu Funicular to connect with Barcelona to Sant Cugat trains.

The other side of the ridge, which the trains go under to the west of Vallvidrera, lies the Vil.la Joana, the country house of the Catalan poet Mossè Jacint Verdaguer (1845–1902). Enquire about opening times.

Funicular station window

63

From the fun park a road leads 6km (4 miles) to the northwest, first through forests and then across the fertile Vallès plain before reaching **Sant Cugat del Vallès**. Many of the town's 30,000 inhabitants work in Barcelona and commute each day by train or car. The main attraction is the monastery, whose origins go back to the Middle Ages. First mentioned in 897, it soon became one of the most important monasteries in Catalonia. The walls probably stand on the ruins of a Roman settlement, in which Bishop Cucophas (Cugat) was executed in 304 on the orders of Emperor Diocletian.

The Benedictine monastery was dissolved in 1835, and the parts that can be seen today stem from the 12th to 17th centuries. A particularly fine artistic achievement is the ★ **Romanesque cloister** by Catell (1190), with its 145 capitals decorated with leaf designs and mythical creatures. Ninth-century tombstones have been discovered under the cloister. Above the simple portal is a large **rose window**, flanked by two smaller ones. The church, with its three aisles, is from the 14th century. Inside the church it is worth taking a close look at the beautiful altar with its picture of the saints by Pere Serra (1375), and the 14th-century tomb of the Abbot Otó. The main apse and two side apses are of Romanesque origin.

Monastery exterior with the rose window, Sant Cugat del Vallès

From Sant Cugat you can drive back via Tibidabo or Cerdanyola (via the A18 motorway), or simply take the regular FGC train.

Montserrat – Terrassa

Montserrat logo

MONTSERRAT

As early as the Middle Ages the Monastery of Montserrat was Spain's second most important shrine – after Santiago de Compostela. Kings, emperors and millions of believers from numerous nations came to pay homage to the Madonna. On the way back from the monastery, it is possible to visit a real jewel of art history – Terrassa, the 'city of the three churches'. Allow a full day for the excursion. Those who want to visit the Montserrat monastery in peace need to start early in the morning, to arrive before the tourist buses. After the cool of the night, you can then experience the mist lifting slowly over the monastery to reveal the glorious sight of the Montserrat mountain.

Alternative routes to Montserrat

A: Take the A7 motorway to Martorell (*see page 72*), and then go a short distance along the N11 before turning off right on the C1411 to Olesa de Monserrat. From here it is only a few kilometres to the station of the Funicular Aeri de Montserrat (the cable cars go up to the monastery every 30 minutes). The road continues to Monistrol. This route can also be used as an alternative way back after coming by route D.

B: Autocars Julià, tel: 93 490 4000. Buses run daily from Sants bus station in Carrer Viriat to the Funicular Aeri de Montserrat (*see below*).

C: By FGC train in the direction of Manresa (journey time 60 minutes) from the Plaça d'Espanya to the Funicular Aeri de Montserrat.

D: Leave Barcelona heading northwest along the Avinguda de la Meridiana and turn off north along the newly-

Sant Cecilia monastery on the way to Montserrat

built A18 motorway in the direction of Terrassa. The turn
off to Terrassa comes after 29km (18 miles). From then on
the motorway is called the Autopista de Montserrat.

On the left-hand side you can already see the massive
★★ **Serra de Montserrat** (The Serrated Mountain). The
characteristic saw-like form of the mountain chain was
caused by erosion. The highest peak is the Turó de Sant
Jeroni at 1,235m (4,050ft). Other notable features are El
Gorro Frigi (Liberty Cap), Les Magdalanes and the Vall
Malalt (Evil Valley), on whose edge the monastery stands
at a height of 725m (2,380 ft). The Serra is also a nature
reserve on account of its rich variety of plants, with more
than 1,500 species.

*The monastery complex on
Serra de Montserrat*

Leave the autopista by the exit Sant Vicenç de Castel-
let/Montserrat and turn left after the toll booth (*peatge*).
After a few minutes you will come to Monistrol. This
village, which used to be somewhat sleepy, has profited
increasingly from the flood of tourists going to Montserrat. From Monistrol, a mountain road serpentines its way
up to the monastery, and the unique quality of this monumental massif soon becomes apparent. After 8km (5
miles) take the turn off to the monastery and you come
to a one-kilometre long row of parking places. Thousands
of people visit the monastery each day in the high season, particularly on Sundays.

Coffee bar on Plaça de la Creu

★ *The Monastery of Montserrat*

A small monastery city has developed around the Plaça de
la Creu (the Square of the Cross), complete with a self-
service restaurant, souvenir shops, a shopping passage
with a bakers' and the monastery information office. On
the left-hand side, where the square goes down steeply,
is a cross (*creu* in Catalan) by Catalan sculptor Josep
Subirachs, dating from 1927, which gave its name to the
square. Looking down into the valley it is possible to see
the middle station of the Funicular Aeri de Montserrat.
The lower station lies south of Monistrol.

Subirachs' cross

From the Plaça de la Creu go along the Baixada de la
Font del Portal. Shortly before reaching the Plaça Abat
Oliba, the 'path of Saint Michael' turns off to the left. Here
there is a memorial to the world-famous Catalan cellist
Pablo (Pau) Casals (1876–1973).

The path ends after about 45 minutes at the Santa Cova
(Holy Cave). According to legend, a figure of the Madonna
of Montserrat was found here. Near the cave is a small
17th-century chapel in which a copy of the statue of the
Virgin is kept. The cave can also be reached by a cable car
which goes up from below the path every 20 minutes from
10am–7pm. On the way you pass a small camping site (tel:
(93) 835 0251) with a wonderful view down into the valley of the Riu Llobregat.

View down to the Holy Cave

The Ermita de Sant Joan

The Finger of God

Above the Camí de Sant Miquel is the cable car station (10am–7pm, every 20 minutes). From the station a 20-minute walk leads to the Chapel of the **Ermita de Sant Joan** (1899). Another possible tour (lasting two hours) leads from the cable car station past a different hermitage up to the peak of Sant Jeroni, with its chapel of the same name. From Sant Jeroni, which is over 1,200m (3,940 ft) high, there is a beautiful ★★ **view** over the entire area.

Back to the Plaça Abat Oliba, lined with shops and accommodation for pilgrims. A market is held here every morning. The market women (*pageses*) from the surrounding area sell their homemade wares, in particular honey (*mel*) and cheese (*formatge*).

From the square, steps lead up to the Via Crucis, the Way of the Cross. Between 1904 and 1919, 14 statues were built. Destroyed during the civil war, they were then created anew by the sculptors Juventeny and Fita. The path is a pilgrimage route to the Chapel of the Holy Virgin (1910) and the Ermita de Sant Miquel, whose chapel dates back to 1870.

A passage joins the Plaça Abat Oliba with the central square of the monastery, the Plaça de Santa Maria. In the background impressive limestone rocks (Peñascos) can be seen, the most striking of which is El Dedo de Deus (The Finger of God).

The square is lined by the monastery buildings, which can look back on a long history. The monastery was founded in 880 in honour of a figure of the Virgin which, according to legend, was found in a nearby cave, the Santa Cova (*see page 65*). In 976 the convent was taken over by the Benedictines. It was extended in the 11th century by monks from the main Benedictine monasteries in Vic and Ripoll, headed by Abbot Oliba. Montserrat then developed into a centre of Christian learning, and an important shrine. In 1522 Ignatius Loyola, founder of the Jesuit order, paid a visit.

In 1808 the complex was sacked and largely destroyed by Napoleon's troops. All that remained from the original complex was the portal of the first Romanesque church and parts of the Gothic cloister (1460). The monks didn't return until 1858 when they rebuilt the monastery. Today, 80 monks live here, organise visits, administer an enormous library and run a book printing and goldsmith's workshop.

Abbot Oliba

On the Plaça de Santa Maria is the Hotel Abad Cisneros (tel: 93 835 0201), remains from the old 15th-century cloister, and a museum, which is in two sections. In the building at the northern end of the square, to the left of the church entrance, is the Department for Early Art, which includes a collection of objects from Egypt and treasures from the Byzantine and Romanesque periods (ceramics, coins, scrolls). The modern department at the southern end of the square contains works by Catalan painters from the last two centuries.

Plaça de Santa Maria

Go through a gateway (built between 1942 and 1968) on the western side of the square and enter the complex of the **Monastery church**. A modern inner courtyard is in front of the Renaissance church which was first built between 1560 and 1592, but has been renovated considerably since then. On the left-hand side is the way to a holy spring and the (closed) entrance to the monastery. The church is 86m (280ft) long, 21m (70ft) wide and 33m (110 ft) high. Its interior design is modern and not particularly interesting. On the right-hand side a door leads from the courtyard to the side aisle. From here you come to the Madonna figure, the patron saint of Catalonia, set above the high altar.

Despite her ornate surroundings, the Virgin is no idealised doll. She is a mysterious mixture of the homely and the hieratic. The head and hands of the wooden statue, which is said to come from the 12th or 13th century, have become black from candle smoke over the years. Hence it is known as ★★ **La Moreneta**, 'The Black Virgin'.

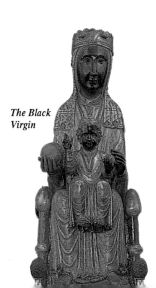

The Black Virgin

The church is famous for its excellent acoustics and the boys' choir from the monastery sings here three times a day. It is the oldest choir in the world, documented as far back as the 13th century. The young singers are taught in their own special school, the *Escolania*. The *Missa Conventual* is at 11am, and the *Salve Regina* at 1pm and 6.45pm (after the vespers). The *Virolai* can also often be heard, a choral work which captures in words and music the Catalans' worship of their 'Virgin of Montserrat': *Rosa d'abril, Morena de la serra, de Montserrat estel…'*.

Sant Pere, Terrassa

Terrassa parish church

Return from the monastery via Monestir on the A18 motorway towards Barcelona. Anyone interested in art history should stop off at **Terrassa**. This town on the bank of the Riu Palau has a population of 150,000 and now lives mainly from its textile industry. The city grew out of the Roman settlement Egara, which itself was built on the foundations of an Iberian town. In the 5th century Terrassa became a diocesan town. It was probably during this period of Visigothic rule that the Sant Miquel chapel was built. This forms the focal-point of an unusual historical collection. In Terrassa's Sant Pere d'Egara district (watch for signs marked *Iglesias visigóticas*), there are three churches built right next to each other. The reason for this was the early Christian belief that the bishop's basilica, the baptistery and the **parish church** should all be next to each other in a closed-off area.

The oldest of the three is the ★ **Sant Miquel** church. This has similarities with the Roman building style (narrow bricks between cubic stones), whilst the ground plan is shaped like a Greek cross, and the shape of the dome can be found in other types of Visigothic and Carolingian churches. Inside the baptistery are ancient columns, Carolingian wall paintings and a Gothic altar by Jaume Cirera and Guillem Talarn.

To the right of Sant Miquel is the ★ **Santa Maria** church, which was built in the 12th century but also includes older elements in the rectangular apses. Among the frescoes, some of which are Carolingian, one in the side apse is particularly interesting. It portrays the murder of Thomas Becket, the Archbishop of Canterbury, in his cathedral (1170). Three years after his death Becket was canonised and revered throughout western Europe. The fresco is proof of the excellent communications in medieval Europe. Also worth looking at is the altar (1460) by Jaume Huguet, one of the last masters of the Catalan high-Gothic style (*see page 42*).

Man and dog, Sant Pere

The **Sant Pere** church consists of a Visigothic transept and choir, whilst the nave is from the 12th century. Inside the church, with its deep recesses and blind arcades in the apses, is an altar by Lluís Borrassà from 1413. Opening times for the church area: Tuesday to Sunday, 9am–1.30pm and 3.30–7.30pm (from October to April only until 6pm).

Now it's time to visit the **Museu Tèxtil Biosca** in the town centre (Parc de Vallparadis). Experts regard this textile museum as one of the finest in the whole of Spain, with collections of priceless treasures, ranging from old Spanish fabrics (including Arabian woven items) to Latin American embroidery.

From Terrassa it is a further 29km (18 miles) back to Barcelona along the A18 motorway.

Excursion 3

Sitges – Vilafranca – Martorell

This 120-km (75-mile) round trip allows you to combine three holiday plans in one: swimming and walking in Sitges, drinking wine in Vilafranca del Penedès and the surrounding area, and studying history in Martorell. The towns are described here in this order, although naturally the tour can also be made in the other direction. For Gaudí fans a visit to Coloma de Cervello is recommended. Here, in the working-class district, is a wonderful church by the modernist maestro.

Sitges holiday resort

Starting from Barcelona take the C246 to Castelldefels. The best exit to take is from Passeig de Colom heading south. The road crosses the Riu Llobregat and comes to the humid La Marina area. On the sea side is the Barcelona-Prat airport. You will reach Castelldefels after about 20km (12 miles). This little town has a population of around 25,000, rising to 30,000 in summer, and contains interesting 10th-century castle ruins and a 7-km (4½-mile) long beach with the usual bars, restaurants and places to play.

From here the route continues up into the mountains. The C246 winds its way up into the Garraf hills, climbing in serpentine curves to 300m (980 ft). There are wonderful panoramic views of picturesque bays and extraordinary rock formations, lashed by the waves of the Mediterranean. After 18km (11 miles) the land becomes flatter again, and ★★ **Sitges**, one of Catalonia's most beautiful resort towns, stretches along two long bays.

Before the war, and indeed even up to the 1950s, this small town was the weekend residence of wealthy Barcelonans. You can still see traces of this time from the palm-lined beach promenade in the southern part of the town. Here there are both elegant city villas from the turn of the century and modern apartment blocks. Most of the ho-

Café Picnic, Sitges

Sitges' parish church

Cau Ferrat

tels are also located in this area, including the Hotel Subur, a pleasant, medium-priced hotel with a view of the sea. Nowadays Sitges is invaded during the high season by tourists, but still regards itself as a cut above the other resorts on the Costa Dorada, the Golden Coast. The golf courses, tennis courts and the yachting harbours all add to this image. In reality, the town is divided into two parts: in the south are the wide beaches, the palm-tree promenade, a pedestrian zone, bars and discotheques. In the north are smaller beaches, the old city centre, more private houses and a less hectic atmosphere. The two parts are divided by a rocky promontory, where the town's history began in the Middle Ages.

The baroque **parish church**, simply called La Punta (The Tip) by the locals, immediately catches the eye. Inside is an interesting altarpiece by Nicolau Credença. Also on the promontory are two interesting museums. The first is the ★ **Cau Ferrat** (Iron Nest), home of painter and writer Santiago Rusiñol (1861–1931), where eccentric meetings of artists are said to have taken place. The interior of the house has more or less been left in its original state, and is full of works by the former owner along with others by El Greco, Picasso and Utrillo. Rusiñol's residence, with its beautiful bays and fountains, is spectacularly situated: the cliffs drop away precipitously beneath the east window to the sea. Opening times: Tuesday to Saturday 10am–1pm and 5–7pm, Sunday 10am–2pm.

Right next to the Cau Ferrat is the Maricel de Mar, a museum located in the palace of the same name. This former hospital was re-designed by the artist Miquel Utrillo. The Pérez Rosales collection includes Romanesque and Gothic paintings, wall paintings by Josep Maria Sert (1874–1945), ceramics and furniture. Opening times are as for the Cau Ferrat.

Sitges has many other attractions to offer visitors, including a rich variety of shops, a lively night life and a third, smaller museum in the old city, the Museu Romàntic in the Casa Llopis, Carrer Sant Gaudenci. This museum has an extensive collection of exhibits from the 19th century and a pretty collection of puppets.

Cafés and shops

Sitges is increasingly developing into a meeting place for homosexuals, particularly around the Carrer Primer de Maig in the south of the city. It has also made a name for itself in the film world with its annual Sitges Festival Internacional de Cinéma de Catalunya in October. Avantgarde theatre is presented during the Festival Internacional de Teatre in April and May.

The quickest way to reach Sitges is by train from the Estació Central-Sants or Passeig de Gràcia in Barcelona. Trains run every 20 minutes from 5.40am–10.30pm, and return every 20 minutes until 10.40pm.

From Sitges the shortest route to Vilafranca (20km/12 miles) is via **Sant Pere de Ribes**. Apart from the castle area (which dates back to 990) and the Romanesque church, the most interesting feature is probably the Gran Casino de Barcelona. This casino, and the adjoining expensive restaurant, are located in a palace built by Eduardo Maristany in 1918. It is open for business every night from 5pm–4am (*see page 91*).

Vilanova i la Geltrú

It is also worth paying a visit to **Vilanova i la Geltrú**. This town of 40,000 inhabitants developed from the medieval centre La Geltrú of 1070. Later, in the 13th century, Vilanova (the new city) was founded. The old fishing quarter is particularly interesting, as are the Santa Maria church (with Renaissance altar), the discoveries from the Roman settlement *Darro*, and the 13th-century Castell de la Geltrú. There are also two museums. The first is the Can Papiol, the former house of artist Joaquim Mir, now transformed into the Museum for 18th-Century Applied Art. With furniture and other items of decoration, the museum gives an excellent insight into life 200 years ago (Tuesday to Saturday 10am–2pm). The second museum is the Museu Belaguer, which includes an Annunciation by El Greco and first-rate paintings by Spanish artists from the 16th to 19th centuries. There is also an archaeological collection and a library. Opening times: Tuesday to Saturday 10am–2pm and 4–7pm, Sunday 10am–2pm.

Can Papiol, Museum for Applied Art

71

From Vilanova i la Geltrú the route continues along the C244 heading north. After passing through Canyelles, you will come to **Odèrdola**. This town was an important bastion in the defence against the Moorish invaders between the 8th and 10th centuries. Graves from pre-Iberian times and remains of an Iberian-Roman settlement can still be seen. The Roman Sant Miquel church is also of interest.

Just 3km (2 miles) away is **Vilafranca del Penedès**. The capital of the Alt-Penedès region has a population of 25,000 and is also Catalonia's number one wine city and home of the Catalan Wine Institute. Three types of grape are grown here: Macabeu, Xarel.lo and Parellada, which all produce excellent white wine. It is possible to taste the wine directly from the barrel in the city's many wine cellars. The wine is drunk from so-called *Porrones*, curious spouted bottles from which it is sprayed into the mouth. The Museu del Vi describes the history of this noble drink from Roman times up to the 15th century. The museum is housed in a Gothic palace (Palau Reial) that was once the residence of the kings of Aragón, and where Pere II died in 1285. It is also worth visiting the City Museum on the upper floor of the same building. Here there is a collection of works by Catalan painters and an exhibition of ceramics and coins. Opening times: Tuesday to Sunday, 10am–2pm and 4.30–7.30pm.

Porron in a bar, Vilafranca

Santa Maria church

Other interesting features in this medieval-influenced town are its numerous palaces, the 13th-century **Santa Maria church** with a group of works by 20th-century sculptor Josef Llimona, the Sant Francesc church (part of a monastery complex) and a small ornithological museum.

The most fascinating time to visit the town is between 29 August and 2 September, when the local festival is held. All over the town people build *castells*, the human towers up to 10m (33 ft) high which are such a popular tradition in this area (*see page 81*). The wine route continues either along the A7 motorway or via the C243 which goes across the extensive wine-growing areas.

Both routes lead to ★ **Sant Sadurní d'Anoia** (13km/8 miles). The sparkling wine industry has changed this little village dramatically over the past century. There are now around 8,500 residents and the village owes its rapid development to a certain Josep Raventós i Domènech. In 1872 he began producing sparkling wine using the famous 'méthode champenoise' which he copied from Dom Perignon in Champagne. Since then the famous *cava* (sparkling wine) of the Raventós family has been sold all over the world under the name 'Codorníu'. Other makes of *cava* from Sant Sadurní have in the meantime also made a name for themselves, but none have such splendid ancestry as Codorníu. The Can Codorníu was built by modernist Josep Puig i Cadafalch (*see page 79*), has a domed hall and is covered in ivy. The appearance may be romantic, but hard work takes place. Bottles are stored for a minimum of nine months, and turned continuously until the dregs have collected in the neck. Finally the dregs are removed and the permanent cork inserted.

From Sant Sadurní take either the motorway or the country road for another 11km (7 miles) to **Martorell**, a town of 16,000 inhabitants. Its symbol is the Pont del Diable or **Devil's Bridge** over the River Llobregat. Legend has it that the bridge was built by Hannibal (218BC). The triumphal arch on the approach to the bridge is said to be in memory of Hannibal's father, Hamilcar Barca, the supposed founder of Barcelona, who fell in Spain in 218BC. In truth, however, the bridge was built by the Romans and extended in the Middle Ages. There are two interesting museums in the town. The Museu Santacana 'L'Enrajolada' was founded by Francesc Santacana (1810–96) and shows Catalan, Hispanic-Arabic and Venetian furnishings, plates, tiles and capitals, and treasures from Romanesque and Gothic churches in the region. The Museu Vicenç, on the other hand, specialises in ceramics and tiles from the 15th to 16th centuries, as well as displaying folkloric and archaeological exhibits from the Baix Llobregat region. Opening times: Tuesday to Saturday, 10am–1pm, Sunday and public holidays 10am–noon.

The home of Codorníu

The Devil's Bridge

Ceramic tiles

In the old hospital of Martorell there is a romantic chapel, whilst the remains of a monastery can be seen around the Santa Margarida church.

From Martorell it is only about 20km (12 miles) along the motorway back to Barcelona. Anyone with time, however, should follow the curves of the C1411 along the right hand side of the Riu Llobregat via Sant Andreu, Pallejà and Sant Vicenç del Horts to ★**Santa Coloma de Cervello**. The reward for the journey is the beautiful grounds of the **Colonia Güell**. The modernist building of the cloth factory and the adjoining settlement were designed in 1898 by Francesc Berenguer, a colleague of Gaudí. The church (built from 1908 onwards) is by the great architect himself, and is a masterpiece of structural engineering. The crypt, main aisle and portico are all supported by completely different types of diagonal columns. The crooked walls give the interior a playful character, as does the constantly changing network of brick ribs. The materials, colours and forms are all suited to the forested landscape. A dim light comes through the delicately-coloured, circular, barred windows. This construction is a lot more rustic and modest and less expressive than Gaudí's works in Barcelona, as if here, for the first time, he was able realise his idea of adapting buildings to nature. Contact the priest in order to arrange a visit.

The Güell settlement can also be reached by FGC train from the Plaça d'Espanya, getting out at Molí Nou.

From Santa Coloma there is a choice of routes back. Either take the A7 motorway or the road via Sant Boi and L'Hospitalet, an industrial suburb of Barcelona with a population of over 350,000.

Colonia Güell

73

The church at Colonia Güell

Art History

Modernism

Modernism is the Spanish – or rather Catalan – version of art nouveau. The idea of turning away from eclectic historicism fell on particularly fertile ground in such an innovation-friendly city as Barcelona. In the middle of the 19th century the city had recovered from the devastating occupation by the Bourbon King Philip V, and was experiencing its *Renaixença* or Renaissance.

Catalan culture began to flourish again after decades of suppression. As a result of its proximity to the Mediterranean and the openness of its economic leaders to new developments, Barcelona experienced a rapid economic upswing during the period of the industrial revolution. One consequence was a sharp increase in the size of the population. The lack of space in the old city became more and more alarming, and so in 1850 it was decided to raze to the ground the remaining city walls, and to build huge ring roads (Rondas) over their foundations.

To the west of the Plaça de Catalunya a completely new district was planned, the Eixample (Spanish *Ensanche*, literally 'expansion', *see pages 46 and 76*). This area became popular with Barcelona's bourgeoisie, and was also a playground for modern ideas. An added factor was that Barcelona was preparing for the 1888 World Exposition. The chosen site, the area of the demolished citadel, presented the architects with the opportunity of starting from scratch and with the challenge of coming up with a new form of creative design.

In spite of certain connections with Spanish Late Gothic and Spanish baroque exuberance and fantasy, from the point of view of style Modernism is essentially original. It represented an attempt to combine new building techniques (using iron and concrete constructions), with elements of the Gothic tradition – a period when Catalonia experienced a cultural boom – and organic forms taken from the natural world. It consisted primarily of the use of natural materials such as ceramics, glass and wood, but in revolutionary combinations. It also involved taking account in the building concept of the characteristics of the Mediterranean area, in terms of climate, light and colours.

Inspired by the natural world

The result was a series of impressive and sometimes bizarre buildings in Barcelona, using ever new forms to seek a synthesis between the technical and artistic possibilities on the one hand, and the desire for optimal living quarters on the other. A planned itinerary, the Ruta del Modernisme, takes in up to 50 key points of Modernist architecture. A multi-ticket, permitting entry to these buildings, can be bought in either the Palau Güell or the Casa Lleó Morera (*see page 47*).

75

L'Eixample

In 1860 a royal decree gave the city planner Ildefons Cerdà (1816–1876) the green light for his plan for a new city. This was to stretch to the west of the Plaça de Catalunya, which was itself to be redesigned. The proposed main axis was the Passeig de Gràcia, which connected the old city to the village of Gràcia. Cerdà's design was revolutionary: wide boulevards were to separate quadratic residential blocks (133m (435ft) by 133m) like the lines on a chess board, but with bevelled corners. Each residential unit was to have green spaces in its inner courtyard, with market places, parks and social facilities around the edge. The height of the buildings was to be limited to four floors and the relationship between the green spaces and the buildings was to be 2 to 1. This gigantic building project gave many young architects the opportunity to put their advanced ideas and experiments into practice.

Passeig de Gràcia

It was primarily the wealthy bourgeoisie who had these exciting new residences built for themselves. Over a period of some 50 years, more than 2,000 buildings of the most modern architectural style went up in and around the new city. More than 50 architects worked on the schemes, although few ever achieved fame beyond the city boundaries. And yet, although glorious and extraordinary art nouveau buildings were created, Cerdà's futuristic and idealistic plans were only partly put into practice. His chessboard pattern did come to fruition, and wide roads were created for cars. But property speculators forced both prices and the height of the buildings sky high: today there are up to eight floors. The green spaces were built over, the social facilities forgotten. Today Eixample is almost as densely populated as the old city. *See Route 5.*

76

Antoni Gaudí (1852–1926)

Antoni Gaudí i Cornet is undoubtedly the most famous of all the fathers of modernism. Like no other, he thought of his art as a life's work and based it on his philosophical and anthropological views. He was eventually successful in his aim of having an anthropological school built next to his main work, the Sagrada Família (*see page 51*). The extreme, individualistic shapes of his buildings, with their elements borrowed from the natural world, can still produce astonishment and cause visitors to stare in shocked silence. There are curved lines inside his buildings as well as on the facades, staircase handrails in the shape of a spine, and, at the Casa Batlló, balconies shaped like Venetian masks. There is also a sense of joyful colour wherever Gaudí has covered large wall and roof areas with mosaics made from tiny pieces of ceramic (*trencadís*).

Casa Batlló balconies

The people of Barcelona had great difficulty making any sense at all of this extraordinary architecture, which didn't leave even the smallest artistic detail to chance. The construction of the Palau Güell (1886–88) stunned the local population while the Casa Milà caused such irritation it was regarded as a disgrace to their beautiful new city. Soon it had a new nickname: La Pedrera, the pile of stones. Even today opinions divide sharply when it comes to Gaudí. For some he is a genius, for others just a dreamer and a highly controversial architect. But it is precisely his versatility and unlimited idealism which make Gaudí – both the person and his works – so interesting.

Casa Milà

Gaudí was born in 1852 in Reus, in the province of Tarragona. His father was a blacksmith and potter, and the son soon learned the technical skills which he was later to employ in his buildings. These skills included the use of small pieces of ceramics and the forging of wrought iron. Gaudí studied architecture in Barcelona until 1878, and the city became his chosen home. His work was honoured for the first time in the design of the Universal Exposition site (the Cascading Fountains, 1875–1881), and through his metal creations (the lanterns at the Plaça Reial, 1878). During his final year of studies he got to know the textile manufacturer Count Eusebi Güell i Bacigalupi. At the world exhibition in Paris Güell had seen Gaudí's design for a glass cabinet for a glove factory in Barcelona. He became the architect's patron and commissioned him to design numerous constructions, including the church for the workers' settlement in Santa Coloma de Cervello (1889–1916). During the construction Gaudí had the chance to carry out a number of experiments in structural engineering. Above all, he was trying to develop vault constructions for large buildings, without the buttresses which are a particular feature of Gothic cathedrals. Where supporting columns were absolutely essential, Gaudí tried to incorporate them into his designs as if they were purely ornamental features.

77

Window, Santa Coloma de Cervello

During his youth Gaudí was very active politically. He was a member of the national comrades movement and in 1878 drew up a plan for a worker-friendly factory. Then in 1883 everything changed. He took over the construction of the Sagrada Família, a project which was to remain an (unfinished) life's work until he died in 1926. In this church he wanted to realise all his dreams: building for the convenience of the people, making use of the forms of the natural world, using natural materials, and putting into practice his new ideas on structural engineering. The church was supposed to stand in a natural balance like a tree. During his final years Gaudí became a curious figure, who walked the streets begging for money for his church. Even today Barcelona's most famous symbol is a point of controversy. Should the basilica be completed or should it be left to stand as an unfinished monument?

Although Gaudí was totally absorbed by his project, in 1920, when he was already an old man, he took to the streets of Barcelona to protest vehemently against the threatening dictatorship. He was arrested, but then quickly set free again. However, he came to a tragic end when he fell under a tram. Because no-one knew who this seriously injured, ragged old man was, he was taken to the hospital for the poor, the Hospital de la Santa Creu, where he died, virtually unnoticed by the wider public.

Gaudí worked almost exclusively in Barcelona. Among the exceptions is the bishops' palace in Astorga in the province of Leon (1887–93). His most important buildings in the Catalan capital are:

Park Güell

Casa Batlló (1904–6), Passeig de Gràcia 43 (*Metro Passeig de Gràcia*). See page 48.

Palau Güell (1886–8), Carrer Nou de la Rambla 3 (*Metro Liceu*). See page 22.

Casa Milà, ('La Pedrera', 1906–10), Passeig de Gràcia 92 (*Metro Diagonal*). See page 49.

Sagrada Família (1883–1926), Plaça de la Sagrada Família (*Metro Sagrada Família*). See page 51.

Park Güell (1900–14), Carrer Olot (*Metro Lesseps*). See page 59.

Finca Güell (1884–7), Avinguda de Pedralbes (Metro Palau Reial).

Casa Vicens (1883–5, privately owned), Carrer Carolines 24 (*Metro Fontana*).

Villa Bellesguard (1900–2), Carrer de Bellesguard 16–20.

Casa Calvet (1898–1902, privately owned), Carrer de Casp 48 (*Metro Urquinaona*).

Col.legi de les Teresianes (1888–90), Carrer de Ganduxer 95–105 (*FGC La Bonanova*).

Colònia Güell (1898–c.1915), Santa Coloma de Cervello (*railway station Molí Nou*). See page 73.

Lluís Domènech i Montaner (1850–1923)

The architectural constructions of Domènech i Montaner can be much more clearly categorised than the works of Gaudí. Whereas Gaudí is said by some to belong to the Expressionist movement, and by others to have been part of Surrealism, Domènech i Montaner is regarded by many critics as the true representative of modernism. His greatest work is without doubt the Palau de la Música Catalana,

Palau de la Música Catalana

which, again in contrast to Gaudí's work, owes part of its brilliance to the efforts of other artists (Arnau, Gargallo). Unlike the chessboard-type pattern of the Eixample district, his Hospital de la Santa Creu i de Sant Pau is characterised by distinctive diagonal lines.

His most important works are:

The Montaner i Simón publishing house (home of the

Tàpies Museum; 1881–86), Carrer Aragó 223 (*Metro Passeig de Gràcia*). See page 48.

Palau de la Música Catalana (1905–8), Carrer Sant Pere més Alt (*Metro Urquinaona*). See page 56.

Castell dels Tres Dragons (1888), Parc de la Ciutadella (*Metro Arc de Triomf*). See page 35.

Hospital de la Santa Creu i de Sant Pau (1902–12), Avinguda Gaudí (*Metro Sant Pau*). See page 52.

Fonda Espanya (1902; in the hotel 'España'), Carrer Sant Pau (*Metro Liceu*). See page 103.

Casa Thomàs (1895–8), Carrer Mallorca 291–293 (*Metro Diagonal*). See page 50.

Hospital de la Santa Creu

Josep Puig i Cadafalch (1867–1957)

The buildings of Puig i Cadafalch – who came from Mataró and was also a politician and a historian – have more of a northern, Gothic flavour. Although designed with enormous detail, they are less clearly delineated stylistically than those of Domènech i Montaner. This can be seen for example at the Casa Amatller, where a variety of different styles are combined.

His most important works are:

Casa Amatller (1900), Passeig de Gràcia 41 (*Metro Passeig de Gràcia*). See page 48.

Casa Martí (1896), Restaurant Quatre Gats, C. Montsió (*Metro Plaça de Catalunya*). See page 86.

Casa Terrades/de les Punxes (1903), Avinguda Diagonal 416–420 (*Metro Verdaguer*). See page 50.

Casa Macaya, (1901), Passeig de Sant Joan 108 (*Metro Verdaguer*). See page 50.

79

Casa Amatller

Casa Terrades

Other jewels of modernism

The Casa Planells (1923–4, Avinguda Diagonal 332) was designed by Josep M. Jujol, an architect who was heavily influenced by Gaudí. Salvador Valeri i Pupurull was responsible for the Casa Comalat (1909, Avinguda Diagonal 442), a somewhat avant-garde construction with a facade in the form of a harlequin's hat. One of the most beautiful art nouveau apothecaries is the Farmàcia J. de Bolós (1904–10, Rambla de Catalunya 77). The building where the London Bar now stands (Carrer Nou de la Rambla 34) was also completed in 1910. Bread and delicious pastries are on offer at the art nouveau bakery Sarret (1898). Even fruit and vegetables can be bought in a modernist ambience. Stands 435–436 in the La Boqueria market (entrance Plaça Gardunya) are so attractive that you may well forget what you wanted to buy. Eroticism is also no stranger to art nouveau interiors. The El Molino variety club (Carrer Vila i Vilà), used to hold its risqué revue show in a building designed by Manuel Joaquim Raspall i Mayol, and completed in 1913.

Festivals and Folklore

The most important festivals

Street festival

Celebrating festivals in Barcelona means, above all, good food, drinking and dancing – and usually all on the streets. It's hard not to let yourself go. You'll find the liveliness and joie de vivre of the otherwise industrious Catalans infectious. For many years a lot of their festivals were forbidden, including the national day, *La Diada* (*see below*). It's not surprising then that many festivals now include an element of celebration of the Catalan national identity.

For a list of public holidays, *see page 97*.

In Barcelona children don't only receive presents at Christmas, but also, and more traditionally, at Epiphany (*Dia dels Reis*). On the evening of **5 January** the arrival of the three holy kings (*Cavalcada de Reis*) is celebrated with a splendid procession which begins at the Columbus Monument by the port.

12 February is the day of Barcelona's patron saint, Santa Eulàlia, who was burned as a witch in 304. During the pre-Lent *Carnaval* period which follows there are numerous processions and street festivals.

In the week before **Easter** (*Semana Santa*) there are a number of special church services, and on Easter Sunday children are given a *mona*, an imaginatively designed chocolate figure.

23 April is the day of the patron saint of Catalonia, *Sant Jordi* (Saint George). A strange custom has grown up this day. Men give a rose to a woman of their choice; women give their sweethearts a book. Everywhere in the city you will see bookstands, so the festival is also known as the 'day of the book'. The day of the female patron saint of Catalonia, the Holy Virgin of Montserrat, is celebrated in more contemplative fashion on **27 April**.

The *Feria de Abril* is an Andalusian rather than Catalonian tradition. It is a form of fair with flamenco performances, put on by Barcelona's southern Spaniards. On the evening of **April 30** there is lively dancing in the streets. The Catalans, in contrast, celebrate the *Festa de Treball*, Labour Day, on 1 May.

Corpus Christi is simply called *Corpus* in Barcelona. On the fountains at the Casa de L'Ardiaca (*see page 30*), and in the cloister of the cathedral, there is a special 'egg dance' – *L'ou com balla*.

Sant Joan on **24 June** is a summer solstice festival. Street festivals take place on the evening before. On Montjuïc an enormous firework display lights up the night.

In July and August the various districts of Barcelona host their own festivals. The most famous event during this time is the *Festa Major de Gràcia* in the week of **15 August**. The *Festival Grec*, a theatre and concert festival, runs for the whole of July at venues all over the city, centred on the Teatre Grec, a small amphitheatre on the slopes of Montjuïc (*see page 43*).

On **11 September**, the Catalan national holiday (*La Diada*), political rallies take place and the Catalan flag, *La Senyera*, with its four red stripes on yellow background, can be seen flying everywhere. In the week of **24 September** Barcelona goes crazy. For four days long the city celebrates its main festival, *La Mercè*, in honour of its other patron saint, Santa Mercedes. Concerts take place in many squares, with cheerful processions.

October is a quieter month, before All Saints (*Tots Sants*) on **1 November**, when people indulge themselves with *castanyades*, roast chestnuts and *panellets*, small marzipan cakes.

On **24 December** the Christmas atmosphere in the city reaches its peak, with markets in front of the cathedral, Christmas vespers, and family feasting.

Instead of playing jokes on each other on 1 April, the Barcelonans do it on **28 December**.

Catalan flag and dancing donkey

Customs

A number of customs, rituals and dances can be found at the large festivals in Barcelona.

Castells: A dangerous custom in which the strong men of the district build a human tower of up to 10m (33ft), which is climbed by a small boy, the *enxaneta* (literally 'weathercock'). Often he falls before reaching the top, sometimes sustaining serious injury. On **24 September** (*La Mercè*) castells are built in the square by the city hall, often reaching to the mayor's balcony.

Correfoc: The *correfoc* go back to history of St George, the dragon-slayer. Noisy groups of animal, devil and horror figures make their way through the city, waving fireworks. The main days for these processions are *Sant Jordi* (23 April) and *La Mercè* (24 September).

Gegants: Each area or district has its own *gegants* (giants), papier-mâché figures up to 3m (10ft) high, representing important figures from the district's history. On **24 September**, the festival of *La Mercè*, the *gegants* from all the districts of Barcelona gather in front of the city hall.

Sardana: This is the Catalan folk dance, whose origins are obscure. The dancers form a circle, join hands and take short steps (*pasos curts*) and long steps (*pasos llargs*) forwards, backwards and to the side. It is a serious affair and the steps are counted. The dancing circle is accompanied by a curious 10-man orchestra, the *cobla*. The *sardana* is an important expression of Catalan autonomy and unity. There are regular *sardana* meetings, for example at the square in front of the cathedral on Saturday at 6.30pm and on Sunday at noon.

Street entertainer

Food and Drink

Catalan food has two roots: the somewhat plain but substantial country cooking (sausage, game, pork dripping, olive oil) and the extensive offerings from the sea. They often combine to make succulent dishes known as *Mar i Montanya* (surf and turf). The fine art of cooking goes back as far as the courts of the kings and counts of the Middle Ages. In 1490 the cookery book *Llibre de Coch* appeared, compiled by Rupert de Nola, the head chef of King Ferdinand of Naples, son of Alfonso of Aragón. The influence of Italian cooking added a variety of pasta dishes to the culinary repertoire. The use of rice, not only in the world-famous paella but in other delicious lesser-known dishes such as *arros negre*, goes back to a Byzantine tradition. The French style of cooking is of more recent influence, having made its way into the local restaurants about 100 years ago.

Breakfast
Breakfast is not a serious matter in Catalonia. The locals just have coffee and either croissants or *churros* (a kind of doughnut). Don't expect too much from breakfast in your hotel: you will probably simply get coffee or tea, white bread, butter and jam. Many modern hotels have a breakfast buffet.

The tapas culture

A much more important part of the culinary timetable in Catalonia, as in the whole of Spain, are the tapas (literally 'lids'), which are eaten between main meals together with a glass of beer or wine. In just about every bar you will find an appetising array of dishes at the counter, ideal if you just want a quick bite.

Among the possibilities are stuffed olives, *anxoves* (anchovies), *tortillas* (omelettes of all sorts), *amanidas* (salads) as well as meat, mushroom and seafood dishes. You will be given a small portion, often on a saucer with just a toothpick to eat with. To drink you can have an aperitif, a glass of sparkling wine or a beer. Tapas are never a main meal, but are an integral part of the bar culture in Spain, in much the same way as crisps or peanuts are in Britain's pubs, but rather more interesting.

Sauces (salsas)
Catalan cooking is characterised by its many sauces. The simplest, and one which is usually eaten cold, is *allioli*, a mixture of garlic and olive oil made into a form of mayonnaise by adding egg yolk. *Romesco*, which comes in many different forms, goes well with salads or grilled dishes. The main elements of this red sauce are olive oil,

Appetising seafood

Crema Catalana

Wine from Penedès

crushed peppers, almonds and garlic. For the creamy *picada* sauce, oil, almonds (and often hazelnuts too), garlic, parsley, and roasted bread are crushed with a pestle and mortar. *Sofregit* is always served warm and consists of braised onions, tomatoes and garlic.

Hors d'oeuvres (entremèses)

There are many types of fresh salad, including *esqueixada* with tomatoes, onions and beans, with shredded salt-cod, or *amanida catalana*, a green salad with sausage and ham. *Xató* comes from Sitges and is a salad with sardines, tuna fish and a *Romesco* sauce. With salad and seafood it is normal to eat *pa amb tomàquet*, a slice of bread, sometimes toasted, coated with olive oil, garlic and crushed tomato. Those who like something a bit more substantial will enjoy *mongetes amb botifarra*, roast pork sausage and beans which have been baked in pork dripping.

Main courses (plat principal)

It is the seafood dishes, however, which can be recommended above all else. *Sarsuela de mariscos* is mixed shell fish. *Supquet de peix*, on the other hand, is a seafood stew. Crayfish and shrimps are eaten *a la plancha* (grilled) or *a la marinera* (steamed) and served with *allioli* or *romesco*. Pure meat dishes include *conill* (rabbit) – which comes with a variety of side dishes, *cargols* (mussels) – or *pollastre* (chicken). Indeed, there are some extraordinary combinations of chicken dishes, including those with crayfish or chocolate sauce. Less extraordinary is the vegetable and meat stew, *escudella de pagès*, or *porc amb ceps* (knuckle of pork).

Puddings (postres)

The Moorish preference for sauces is also obvious from Catalonia's selection of puddings. *Crema Catalana*, a delicate dish made from eggs, milk and sugar, is not for those who are counting their calories. *Menjar blanc* is also sweet and consists of ground almonds and milk. As an alternative try one of the many local cheeses, made from sheep or goat's milk. In the cheaper restaurants you will often simply be served yoghurt or fruit.

Drinks

Beer (*cervesa*) is becoming increasingly popular. The wide range of Catalan wines can also be highly recommended. In Catalonia there are eight official wine-growing areas. *Priorato* is a good red table wine from the Tarragona region. Also from this region, as well as from Allela, comes *Falset*, a good white wine. The rosé wine, *Trepat*, comes from the Penedès area, whilst the Costa Brava sun gives *Garnatxa* its sweet, fruity taste. Cheaper, but often ex-

cellent, are the house wines (*vi de casa*) which can be found in just about every restaurant. The sparkling wines (*cava*) of the region come from the area around Sant Sadurní and have made a name for themselves all over the world. The dry wines, *Brut* and *Brut nature* are particularly good. Coffee is drunk either black (*café sol*), with a little milk (*tallat*), with a lot of milk (*amb llet*) or diluted with added water (*café americàno*).

Sangria, made with wine, lemon juice and soda

Restaurants

People in Barcelona eat much later than in most European countries. The midday meal is between 2–5pm and the evening meal between 9pm and midnight. Each restaurant is obliged to offer a fixed price menu (*menu del dia*) which usually consists of three courses and is the cheapest way to eat. But Barcelona can offer culinary delights to suit all tastes and every budget. Note that many restaurants are closed on Sunday evening and/or Monday, and that it is worth making a booking beforehand.

A selection of recommended Catalan restaurants:
Around 5000 Ptas: In Gràcia there is the high-class **Botafumeiro**, offering Galician seafood (Mayor de Gràcia 81, tel: 93 218 4230). **Neichel** (Avinguda Pedralbes 16, tel: 93 203 8408) and **Reno** (Carrer Tuset 27, tel: 93 200 9129) are also both excellent.

  Around 3000 Ptas: Also popular among the locals is **Agut d'Avignon** (Trinitat 3, tel: 93 302 6034). **Set Portes** (Passeig Isabel II 14, tel: 93 319 3046), with its art nouveau interior, and **El Túnel** (Pto Olímpico, tel: 93 221 0290) are also classics. Slightly run-down, but full of tradition (since 1835) is the rustic **Los Caracoles** (Escudillers 14, tel: 93 302 3185). Situated in a dark side-street off the Ramblas, it used to be a meeting point for artists. **La Masia del Tibidabo** (Plaça del Tibidabo 1, tel: 93 417 6350)

A meal starts with pa amb tomàquet

Set Portes Restaurant

Gambrinus Restaurant

offers its guests a wonderful view over the city. **Peixe-rot Barcelona** (Tarragona 177, tel: 93 424 6969) specialises in seafood. **Gambrinus** can be recognised by the huge king prawn which has become the symbol of the newly renovated Moll de la Fusta (tel: 93 221 4031).

Around 2000 Ptas: In these restaurants the quality of the food is often more impressive than the interior decoration. Good recommendations in the old city include: **Agut** (Gignàs 16, tel: 93 315 1709); the **4 Gats**, in an art nouveau building by Puig i Cadafalch and a popular meeting point for artists such as Picasso around the end of the last century (Carrer Montsió 3, tel: 93 302 4140); the **Amaya**, which is named after a famous flamenco dancer (Rambla Santa Mònica 20, tel: 93 302 1037); and the **Compostela** (Carrer de Ferran 30, tel: 93 318 2317). The **Garduña** (Carrer Morera 17, tel: 93 302 4323) in the La Boqueria market is famous for its fish dishes.

Vegetarian restaurants in all price categories are becoming increasingly popular. **Illa de Gràcia** (Carrer Sant Domènec 19, tel: 93 238 0229) has excellent food, whilst **Self Naturista** (Carrer de Santa Anna 11, tel: 93 318 2378) in the old city is more a place to get a snack.

Self-catering and markets
The best option if you are catering for yourself is to visit the markets. The most famous, but not necessarily the cheapest, is the Mercat Sant Josep (La Boqueria, *see page 19*) on the Ramblas. More traditional are the Mercat de Concepció (Carrer d'Aragó), Mercat Sant Antoni (Carrer Comte d'Urgel) and the Mercat Santa Catarina (Avinguda de Francesc Cambó 16). Supermarkets now have a wide range of produce, and small *colmados* (corner shops), which offer a more personal service, can be found all over the city.

Vegetable market

86

Shopping

Department stores and shopping malls

El Corte Inglés on Plaça de Catalunya is the town's busiest department store with other branches in Diagonal and in the nearby Portal de l'Angel, a lively shopping street running down from the Plaça de Catalunya towards the cathedral. Department stores have been superseded by shopping malls and galleries, of which **Bulevard Rosa** remains one of the best. **The Drugstore**, at Passeig de Gràcia 71, and **VIPs** in the Rambla de Catalunya have shops and cafés. Commercial centres such as L'Illa (Diagonal) and El Triangle (Plaça Catalunya) offer a wide range of shops.

El Corte Inglés

Fashion in Bulevard Rosa

Eixample

This is where to shop for designer clothes and furniture. Names to look out for include Roser Marcé, José Font, Luz Diaz, Jordi Cuesta, Chu Uroz and Lourdes Vergara. Chain stores include **Massimo Dutti**, **Mango** and **Zara** (for kids as well).

Passeig de Gràcia

No 35, **Loewe**, has smart leatherware. No 55, **Bulevard de Rosa**, with some 70 shops, is a classy designer shopping mall, mostly selling fashion clothes. Also at 55 is **Centro Permanente de Artesania**, which shows new local craft work. No 89, **Adolfo Dominguez**, is a leading designer of classic fashion. No 96, **Vinçon**, is the most stylish interior design store.

Rambla de Catalunya

No 100, **Groc**, is the home of Barcelona's fashion king, Toni Miró, and the shop was a trailblazer when it opened in the late 1960s. There are several high-class fashion and shoe shops on this pleasant street.

Roselló

No 275, **Dos y Una** is an up-market souvenir shop. No 271, **La Inmaculada Concepción** sells Modernist fixtures and fittings in a corner of a former Modernist home. No 277, **Joaquin Berao**, has an art nouveau interior where jewellery is sold. No 197, **Camilla Hamm**, has early 20th-century furniture and also acts as an art gallery.

Diagonal

No 376, **D Barcelona** is a fun design shop with sculptures, watches and repro radios. No 403, **Pilma**, is a designer furniture shop also selling objets d'art. No 466, **Eleven**, is a shoe shop with a striking modern interior by Manuel Ybarguengoitia and Maria del Mar Nogués. No 469, **Jean**

A shop in the Call

Pierre Bua, with a metal and concrete interior by Eduard Samsó, is where to find all Spain's top designer names. **Sara Navarra**, at No 598, is good for inexpensive shoes and leatherware.

Barri Gòtic
This is where to look for antiques, second-hand books, ceramics and young fashion.

Freneria: No 1, **Grafiques el Tinell**, specialises in old prints and lithographs. Also at No 1 is **La Caixa de Fang** selling jars, jugs, plates and casseroles.

Banys Nous: No 5, **Gemma Povo**, stocks antiques including wrought iron, furniture and hand-blown glass. In Carrer de Call go to **La Roda** for earthenware and decorated ceramics and **Obach i Obach** for hats.

Plaça de Sant Josep Oriol: Molsa has ceramics ancient and modern. In neighbouring Plaça del Pi is the **Montforte** toy shop. Carrer Peritxol, off Plaça del Pi, is full of art galleries (Dalmau, Picasso and Miró's agent, operated from here). No 2, Libreria Quera, is the place to go for maps and photography books about Catalonia.

88

Ceramic stall

Markets
The big flea market is **Els Encants** in Plaça de les Glorièss Catalanes (Metro Lines I and II). It's fun and there are some bargains to be found. Open Monday, Wednesday, Friday and Saturday from 8am–8pm, 7pm in winter.

A small **antiques market** is held in the cathedral square on Thursdays, and painters sell their works on Sundays in Plaça Sant Josep Oriol. A **stamp and coin market** is held in Plaça Reial just off the Rambla from 10am–2pm on Sunday. Stamps and books are in Sant Antoni market, west of the Rambla at the far end of the Carrer del Carme, (10am–2pm on Sunday).

Plaça Sant Josep Oriol

Nightlife

The wealth of attractions means that a night in Barcelona can easily last until the next morning, particularly as people start their evenings a lot later than in most European countries. A typical programme is to eat at around 10pm, then go to a bar, and finally at around 1 or 2am visit a disco, variety show or whatever. Theatre performances often don't start until 10pm, whilst cinemas have their last showing at 10.30pm or even 1am.

Night on the town

There are no really typical entertainment areas in the city, although certain general distinctions can be made.

Those interested in night shows, striptease or erotic variety shows should take a stroll along the Avinguda del Paral.lel. The Barri Xinès around the Carrer Nou de la Rambla, which used to be full of bars and nightclubs, can no longer be recommended. It has fallen into decay and been passed by in the city's development plans. Crime and prostitution are now so widespread here that it is not even advisable to take an evening walk in this area.

Sign of a good time

It is, however, still worth taking an evening stroll along the Ramblas. The atmosphere around midnight at the Rambla Santa Mónica and the nearby Plaça Reial should not be missed. Things are quieter and more contemplative in the Barri Gòtic and in Casc Antic, north of the Via Laietana. Those with high expectations won't be disappointed by the Eixample district on both sides of the Passeig de Gràcia, even if one does have to pay somewhat more here for a beer or a cocktail than you would in bars in the old city centre.

Cabaret

The Gràcia district, which has maintained its provincial character, is becoming increasingly popular. Incorporated into Barcelona in 1897 it is now the home of many students and artisans and a large part of the city's alternative scene. During the day the Carrer Gran de Gràcia is the business centre. At night, the lights go on in the many beautiful squares in the area: at the Plaça de Diamant (with its memorial to the Catalan writer Mercè Rodoreda; at the Plaça Ruis i Taulet (also known as the Plaça del Rellotge due to its clock tower in the middle of the square); and at the Plaça del Sol which has an original sun dial. The top spots in Gràcia are the so-called music bars, where disc jockeys spice the passionate pub discussions with equally hot music.

Discotheques can be found all over the city, and there are often large distances between the top venues. But one thing is certain: nothing gets going before 1am, so you need plenty of stamina. There is also a wide range of live music on offer, including many foreign groups, whilst in the old city there are a number of interesting live clubs which specialise in jazz.

Cinemas

The Catalans are enthusiastic cinema-goers. Long queues are common, particularly for the large Hollywood productions. But an independent Catalan film culture is also developing rapidly. The following cinemas show films either in their original versions or with sub-titles:

Filmoteca de la Generalitat de Catalunya, Av de Sarrià 33, tel: 93 410 7590 (*FCG 134 Sarrià*) specialises in original versions of foreign films at low prices. Performances at 6pm, 8pm and 10pm.

Verdi, Salas 1–5; Verdi 32 (Gràcia), tel: 93 237 0516 (*Metro Fontana*). Last performance 10.30pm. After midnight on Friday and Saturday.

Icaria-Yelmo (Metro Vila Olímpica, tel: 93 221 7585). Fifteen screens to choose from, all VO (original version).

Theatres/concerts

The musical theatres are particularly interesting for foreign visitors. World-renowned for opera is the **Gran Teatre del Liceu** (*see page 21*), Rambla 61, tel: 93 485 9913 (*Metro Liceu*). Another unforgettable experience is a concert in the art nouveau palace, **Palau de la Música Catalana** (*see page 56*), Amadeu Vives 1, tel: 93 268 1000 (*Metro Urquinaona*). If you are interested in Catalan theatre try the **Teatre Nacional de Catalunya**, tel: 93 232 7436, **Romea** (Hospital 51, tel: 93 301 5504), **Poliorama** (Rambla dels Estudis 115), tel: 93 317 7599, **Lliure** (Montseny 47, tel: 93 218 9251) or **Mercat de les Flors** (Leida 59, tel: 93 426 2102), which also has visiting companies.

Bars

Barcelona has bars of every conceivable type, from classy cocktail bars to new-wave establishments and student dives. Bars are places for the neighbourhood to gather together, although when a new bar becomes the talk of the town, guests come from all over the city to test it out. The following is a subjective list of interesting bars:

Boadas Cocktail, Carrer dels Tallers 1 (*Metro Plaça de Catalunya*). Barcelona's oldest cocktail bar. Classy but not overly chic. Just around the corner in Carrer de les Sitges is continental Europe's only whisky museum, the Taberna Escocesa (the Scottish Tavern).

Nick Havanna, Roselló 208 (*Metro Diagonal*). An absolute must for those who love to drink in a chic atmosphere. One of the first "designer bars". Open till 8am.

Samba Brazil, Lepanto 297 (*bus 17*). In the evening the crowds flock to this small cocktail bar. Brazilian specialities with lots of sugar and lots of alcohol

Snooker Club Barcelona, Roger de Llúria 42 (*Metro Passeig de Gràcia*). Here you can sip a cocktail then play billiards. Next door is the classy Ticktacktoe restaurant.

Poliorama theatre

The chic Nick Havanna

Café de l'Opera, Rambla 74 (*Metro Liceu*). One of the best meeting places on the Ramblas morning, noon and night.

London, Nou de la Rambla 34 (*Metro Liceu*). A basic beer pub, but with many interesting guests.

Eldorado, No 4 Plaça del Sol (*Metro Fontana*). A music bar at the main meeting point in Gràcia. Young clientele and post-modern atmosphere. Excellent music.

Café de l'Opera

Discotheques

Disco entrance prices start at around £12.

Otto Zutz, Lincoln 15 (*Metro Plaça Molino*). Classy disco, for tie-wearers only. Live concerts.

Zeleste, Almogàvers 122 (*Metro Marina*). Salsa hall, punk bar and large dance floor with video – a paradise for disco-lovers. Wear whatever you like. Live concerts.

Karma, Plaça Reial (*Metro Liceu*). Gets like a sauna at around 3am. Good music of all types.

KGB, Alegre de Dalt 55 (Gràcia) (*Metro Joanic*). Black is in here. Good music and live concerts.

Psicódromo, Almogàvers 86 (*Metro Marina*). A psycho-trip in a factory building. Starts in the early morning.

One of the latest night spots is Maremagnum, the commercial centre in the port, with various bars from salsa to jazz.

The Karma disco

Dancing clubs

There are still a number of dancing clubs with their own orchestras, for those who want to fox-trot and dream.

La Paloma, Tigre 27 (*Metro Universitat*). Gold-plated balustrades, low lights, a man in a glitter suit singing a heart-rending tango. For nostalgia lovers only.

Variety and other shows

Barcelona's fame is not built on variety shows, but here are a couple of venues:

Arnau, Paral.lel, 60

Barcelona City Hall, Rambla de Catalunya,2-4.

Jazz clubs

Barcelona has a thriving, innovative jazz scene with many new bars. Check local listings.

Harlem, Carrer Comtessa de Sobradíel 8 (*Metro Liceu*). Meeting point for the local jazz scene. Free entrance.

Jamboree, Plaça Reial 17. Regular concerts.

La Bôite, Avda. Diagonal 477.

Advertising for jazz

Casino

Those with money to gamble away can visit the **Gran Casino de Barcelona**. In neo-classical style with a high class restaurant, it is near Sitges. Sant Pere de Ribes, road C 246, tel: 93 893 3666.

Getting There

Climate – when to go

The best months to visit Barcelona are May and June, when the rising temperatures (average 20°C) encourage people outdoors again, and September and October when the sea is still a very pleasant 20°C for swimming.

Fun at the beach

In winter the temperature seldom falls below zero, but the weather can often be cool and rainy – not exactly ideal for looking around the city. The oppressively hot summer months are not really conducive to sightseeing, either. At this time you will find the city in a somewhat sleepy mood, as the locals either head off to the beaches or retire to the cool of their homes.

School holidays in Catalonia last almost 3 months, from the middle of June to the beginning of September, and Barcelonan families leave the city if they can with the breadwinners sometimes joining them at weekends, so the city is not overcrowded.

By car

The French border is 149km (92 miles) north at La Jonquera on the A7 motorway. The toll amounts to around 1,500 Ptas. Avoid Friday night and Sunday evening rush-hours. The Royal Automobile Club of Catalunya is manned 24 hours. It is at Diagonal 687, tel: 93 495 5000 or 900 365 505 (24 hr assistance).

93

By train

The main RENFE stations are França terminal by the port and Sants station towards the south (RENFE is the national railway network). Many trains, however, go through the city. If they do, it may be more convenient to get off at Passeig de Gràcia or Plaça de Catalunya. For all rail enquiries, tel: 93 490 0202 (national) or 93 490 1122 (international).

Train crossing

By plane

Barcelona airport (for information, tel: 93 298 3838) is situated 12km (7 miles) south of the city at El Prat. Iberia is the national carrier and there is a shuttle service operating from here to the capital, Madrid. The airport houses a tourist office, bank, car-hire facilities and a hotel reservation service. The main Iberia office is in Carrer Diputació 258. For international reservations tel: 902 400 500.

A smooth, efficient bus service, the Aerobús, runs every 15 minutes between the airport and Plaça Catalunya, and vice versa, stopping at Sants and other strategic places en route. It takes about 35 minutes. There are also trains to Sants and Plaça Catalunya.

Getting Around

Cars and car hire

In view of the enormous volume of traffic, touring the city by car is not to be recommended. It's much better to use the underground, buses or taxis. Apart from anything else, this way you avoid the desperate problem of finding a parking space. In the city centre there are virtually no free parking places, and meters are expensive. Parking on pavements with yellow markings is strictly forbidden; offending cars will immediately be towed away. Should you manage to find a parking space (avoid dark side streets) it is advisable to take all your valuables with you, as car break-ins are part of normal daily life in Barcelona. The safest option, although expensive, is to use the underground car parks.

If you want to hire a car for trips outside the city, tourist offices will direct you to rental companies, or they can be contacted at the airport. Rates are lower outside the high season. The minimum age for renting a car varies between 19 and 21, and your driving licence must have been valid for more than a year.

For information and help contact: Reial Automòbil Club de Catalunya (RACC), tel: 93 495 5000.

Waiting for the train

Underground (Metro)

Barcelona has an excellent metro system (*see Map on page 94*), whose five lines (each colour coded) reach nearly every interesting sight in the city and now link up with the FGC network. At each station the directions of the trains are clearly signposted. Trains run from 5am–11pm during the week and until 1am at weekends and holidays though there are plans to extend the timetable. The last metro is signalled by a hooter as it comes into the station.

Bus

Barcelona's bus timetable is not easy to understand, but once you have got used to the system, it will save a number of long trips on foot from the Metro stations – and it's fun to cross the city overground, at least outside rush hour.

Night buses (*Nit bus*) run on the main routes every half an hour until 4am.

Bus turístic (No 100, from Easter to January). Two bus routes (*Ruta Nord* and *Ruta Sud*) start at the Plaça de Catalunya and make a two-hour trip via the main sights of the city. You can interrupt your journey at any point.

Bus turístic

Train

The lines of the Ferrocarrils de la Generalitat (FGC) complement the Metro in the greater Barcelona area. The main junction is Plaça de Catalunya. From here the line C1 goes

95

to El Prat Airport (6am–10.30pm, every 30 minutes).

The national trains of the state railway company RENFE go from the Estació Central-Sants station, or Estació de França (*see page 93*).

For information about public transport, tel: 93 318 7074 (metro) or 93 205 1515 (FGC) or 010. Information, timetables, books of tickets and tourist tickets – both of which are considerably cheaper than single tickets – are all available at the counters in the stations or the information office in Plaça Universitat metro.

Taxi stand, Sants station

Taxi

More than 9,000 of these yellow and black 'ants' add to the city's traffic jungle. Late at night, in particular, they can be the only means of transport available. A green light on top of the car means that it is free. Taxis stop if you flag them down. There are also taxi stands at a number of key locations and at the main hotels. Taxis are not too expensive, and the fare is shown on a meter. A tip is always appreciated.

Talulat Taxi company, tel: 93 300 3811. Radio-Taxi, tel: 93 330 0808 or 93 322 2222.

Other means of transport

Interesting ways of travelling include the funicular railways to Montjuïc, Tibidabo and Vallvidrera, and the Transbordador Aeri (cable car, Tuesday to Sunday) from Montjuïc over the port to Barceloneta. Barcelona's last tram, the Tramvia Blau, shouldn't be forgotten, either.

For information (and bookings) for trips to Mallorca and the other Balearic islands contact Compañía Trasmediterránea, Est. Marítima, Muelle de San Beltrán, C. P. 08039, tel: 93 443 25 32.

Funicular railway

Facts for the Visitor

Travel documents

All non-Spaniards require a passport or identity card. Visas are needed by non-EU nationals, unless their country has a reciprocal arrangement with Spain.

Customs

Non-EU members can bring 400 cigarettes, one bottle of spirits, two of wine, 50g of perfume; EU-members have guide levels of 800 cigarettes, 10 litres of spirit and 90 litres of wine. Customs keep a close watch for drugs, which are illegal.

Currency regulations

There is no limit on the amount of pesetas or foreign currency you can bring into Spain. The maximum that can be taken out is 100,000 Ptas. Up to 500,000 Ptas worth of foreign currency, or the amount you declared on arrival, can be taken out.

Motorists

A car is completely unnecessary in Barcelona, as already stressed (*see page 95*). If you do drive, a map of the city is essential. These are supplied by the tourist offices, who continually update their information pamphlets.

Street signs

97

Information

Information kiosk

Information and brochures can be obtained from Spanish tourist offices:

In the UK: The Spanish Tourist Office, 22–23 Manchester Square, London W1M 5AP, tel: 0171 486 8077.

In the US: 666 Fifth Avenue, New York. NY 10022, tel: 265 8822.

In Barcelona, an excellent information centre has opened underneath Plaça Catalunya, it also offers a ticket-buying service and bank. Tel: 93 304 3135. From 9am–9pm. Also a telephone information service 010 ought to be able to answer any questions, in English too. Other information offices are at the airport; Central-Sants railway station; City Hall, Plaça de Sant Jaume; Palau de la Virreina, La Rambla 99; and Poble Espanyol, Montjuïc.

On Catalonia: Palau Robert, Passeig de Gràcia 107. Tel:93 238 4000.

Public holidays

1 January; 6 January (Epiphany); 19 March (St Joseph); Good Friday; Easter Monday; 1 May; Ascension Day; Corpus Christi; 24 June (Midsummer's Day); 29 June (Saints Peter and Paul); 25 July (St James); 15 August (Assumption); 11 September (Catalan national holiday); 24

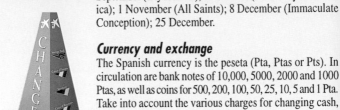

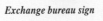

Bureau de Change office

Exchange bureau sign

Newspapers in Spanish and Catalan

September (city festival); 12 October (Discovery of America); 1 November (All Saints); 8 December (Immaculate Conception); 25 December.

Currency and exchange

The Spanish currency is the peseta (Pta, Ptas or Pts). In circulation are bank notes of 10,000, 5000, 2000 and 1000 Ptas, as well as coins for 500, 200, 100, 50, 25, 10, 5 and 1 Pta. Take into account the various charges for changing cash, cheques and using credit cards. With most credit cards you can obtain cash 24 hours a day at many cashpoint machines.

Banks are open Monday to Friday 8.30am–1 or 2pm. Money changing offices are open longer (until 10 or 11pm) in the Central-Sants railway station and the airport.

Tipping

Even when service is included it is normal to gives waiters and taxi drivers a tip of around 10 percent. Between 50 and 100 Ptas is also normal for each piece of luggage carried for you. For shoe-cleaners, cloakroom attendants and ushers around 25 Ptas is usual.

Media

Foreign newspapers can be bought on the day of publication at the kiosks on the Ramblas. Here you can also buy a weekly guide, *Guia del Ocio*, which tells you what's on. The main Spanish newspapers are *El Pais, La Vanguardia* and *El Periódico* (including extensive listings). *Avui* and *El Periódico* are published in Catalan.

Language

So many people from other parts of Spain live in Barcelona that Castilian (Spanish) is often a safer bet than the local Catalan. Be that as it may, a Catalan phrasebook will certainly come in very handy.

Museums
Museums are generally closed on Monday and in the afternoon on Sunday and public holidays. Check with individual museums for opening hours.

Shops
Shops are normally open 9am–1pm, 4.30–7 or 8pm, department stores 10am–9 or 9.30pm.

Markets
Antiques market: Avda. de la Catedral, Thursday 9am–8pm.

Books and coins: Mercat Sant Antoni, Sunday 10am–2pm.

Flea market: El Encants, Plaça de les Glòries, Monday, Wednesday, Friday and all day Saturday.

Art: Plaça Sant Josep Oriol, Saturday 11am–8.30pm, Sunday 11am–2.30pm (not August).

Plaça Sagrada Família, Saturday, Sunday, public holidays 10am–3pm.

Numismatist and Philatelist market: Plaça Reial, Sunday 10am–2pm.

Food markets, *see page 86*.

Postal services
The main post office is in Plaça Antoni Lopez in the port area, tel: 93 216 0453. Open Monday to Friday 9am–9pm, Saturday 9am–2pm.

Other post offices (*correu*) are open in the mornings only. Stamps can be bought at tobacconists (*tabacs*) which have yellow and red signs.

Telephone
Phone booths take 5, 25 and 100 peseta coins, as well as phone cards sold in tobacconists, and are suitable for international calls.

To dial Barcelona from abroad use the code for Spain code (34) followed by that for Barcelona (3). Note that since April 1998, all numbers in the province of Barcelona have begun with 93. From Barcelona the international operator for Europe is 008, for the rest of the world 005. To call abroad, first dial the international access code 07, then the relevant country code: Australia 61; France 33; Germany 49; Italy 39; Japan 81; Netherlands 31; United Kingdom 44; United States and Canada 1.

Time
Spain is six hours ahead of US Eastern Standard Time and one ahead of Greenwich Mean Time.

99

Public telephones

Medical help and chemists

Visitors from the EU have the right to claim health services available to the Spanish. UK visitors should obtain form E111 from the Department of Health prior to departure. However, it is advisable to take out private health insurance before you start your holiday. In an emergency go to the *Urgencias* (accident) departments at any of these three hospitals:

Hospital Sant Pau, Domènech's Modernista hospital up behind the Sagrada Família in Carrer Sant Antoni Maria Claret 167, tel: 93 436 4711. Hospital de la Creu Roja, opposite in the Carrer del Dos de Maig 301, tel: 93 440 7500. Hospital Clinic, over towards Sants station, at Carrer de Casanova 143, tel: 93 323 1414.

Dentist: Clíníca Jasnos, Carrer de Muntaner 375 60 2a, tel: 93 200 2333. Open daily 9am–1.30pm, 4–8.30pm.

Chemists are open until 8pm. Information about chemists which are open at night can be found in the daily newspapers. (For emergency numbers, *see below*)

Crime

Crime in Barcelona is no more frequent than in any other large city. Nevertheless the following tips are worth heeding: never leave anything valuable in your car; never carry more money than necessary; leave your passport at the hotel and take a copy with you; take care when getting money out of cashpoint machines; wear handbags and cameras across your body.

Lost property

Main office: Servei de Troballes, at Carrer Cintat 9, tel: 93 402 3161.

In the event of theft or loss of your wallet or luggage, there is a chance of recovering at least your documents. Thieves are generally only interested in money or other valuables.

Emergency numbers

Police: tel: 091; *Guardia Urbana* (city police) tel: 092.

Twenty-four hour police help-line, with interpreters available: tel: 93 290 3000, La Rambla 43

Emergency doctor: tel: 93 212 8885, 255 5555

Ambulance: tel: 061 (city service), tel: 300 2020 (Red Cross).

Fire Service: tel: 080

Embassies and consulates

United Kingdom: Avinguda Diagonal 477, tel: 93 419 9044.

United States of America: Pg. Reina Elisenda 23, tel: 93 280 2227.

Accommodation

Hotels

Welcoming hotel sign

Welcoming hotel sign

Even after the Olympic Games, which caused a rush of building activity to accommodate all the visitors, there is still a shortage of hotels and it is best to book early, particularly in medium-priced hotels in good locations. For general information, tel: 93 301 6240.

Hotels in Spain are classified into five categories (from one star to five stars). *Hostales* are generally more basic and can be either one star or two stars.

In this guide hotels are grouped as follows:

$$$$* luxury hotels; *$$$* first class hotels; *$$* good hotels; *$ basic hotels.

Most of the hotels listed are located centrally, in or around the old city. There is generally quite a price difference between high- and off-season. Single rooms cost around 60–80 percent of a double room. Breakfast in Spain is always charged for separately and costs between 600 and 2000 Ptas extra.

102

$$$$ (30,000–60,000 Ptas)
Le Meridien, No 111 Ramblas, tel: 93 318 6200. This luxury hotel was renovated in 1989 and has every modern comfort.

Husa Palace, Gran Via de les Corts Catalanes 668, tel: 93 318 5200; and **Princesa Sofía**, Plaça Pius XII 4, tel: 93 330 7111. Both meet the highest international hotel standards.

Hotel Oriente

$$$ (14,000–30,000 Ptas)
Colón, Avinguda Catedral 7, tel: 93 301 1404. The best hotel in this category. To enjoy the wonderful view over the cathedral you have to put up with a certain amount of noise from the traffic.

Rialto, Carrer de Ferran 42, tel: 93 318 5212. Modern.
Oriente, Ramblas 45–47, tel: 93 302 2558. For those who like something traditional. A little run down, but with history, having been here since 1930.

Majestic, Passeig de Gràcia 70–72, tel: 93 488 1717. Classy and tasteful.

The classy Majestic

$$ (5000–20,000 Ptas)
San Agustín, Plaça Sant Agustí 3, tel: 93 318 1658. Quiet and yet still at the centre of things, just 200m from the Ramblas.

There are two good hotels in a quiet street off La Rambla: **Cortés**, 25 Carrer de Santa Anna, tel: 93 317 9112 and **Cataluña**, 24 Carrer de Santa Anna, tel: 93 301 9150.

Mesón de Castilla, Valldoncella 5, tel: 93 318 2182. A well maintained establishment on the edge of the old town.

Suizo, Plaça de l'Àngel 12, tel:93 310 6108. On the edge of the Barri Gòtic, atmospheric and full of tradition.

$ (4,000–12,000 Ptas)
In this category you have to be prepared to forgo certain comforts.

España, Carrer Sant Pau 9–11, tel: 93 318 1758. Although the hotel is not the most modern and is in a somewhat dubious area, it has its attractions, having been designed by art nouveau architect Domènech i Montaner. The dining room is particularly beautiful.

Nouvel, Carrer de Santa Anna 18–20, tel: 93 301 8274. Art nouveau atmosphere.

Jardí, Plaça Sant Josep Oriol 1, tel: 93 301 5900, and **Condal**, Boqueria 23, tel: 93 318 1882. Both are good value, clean and well situated.

Pensions

These most basic establishments are generally not to be recommended. Prices range from 800 to 2000 Ptas a night. However, for those on a tight budget, who are prepared to share a room if necessary and aren't too bothered about having a quiet night, there are a number of possibilities including:

Colón 3, Carrer Colón (Plaça Reial), tel: 93 318 0631, or **Oasis II**, Plaça del Palau 17, tel: 93 319 4396.

Youth hostels

Prices are between 1,200 and 2,275 Ptas per night. In the high season, beds should be booked well in advance:

Casal de Joves, Passeig de Pujades 29, tel: 93 305 2004; **Verges de Montserrat**, P. Marc de Déu del Coll 41–51, tel: 93 210 5151; **Pere Tarrés**, Numancia 149–151, tel: 93 410 2309; **Studio**, Duquessa d'Orleans 58, tel: 93 205 0961.

103

The Hotel Suizo

Index

Antic Hospital de la
Santa Creu 19
Aquarium 33
Arc de Triomf..............36

Barcelona Chair 41
Barcelona
Tourist Office 47
Barceloneta 38, 45
Barri Xinès 21

Café de l'Opera 21
Carrer Ample..............33
Carrer Montcada 37
Casa Amatller.............48
Casa Batlló 48
Casa de l'Ardiaca 30
Casa de la Caritat 18
Casa de la Ciutat 26
Casa de la Pia
Almoina.................29
Casa dels Canonges 26
Casa Joan Coma 49
Casa Josep
Ferrer-Vidal............50
Casa Leo Morera........47
Casa Macaya 50
Casa Manuel
Margarida................46
Casa Marfà 49
Casa Milà 49
Casa Pilar Basols........50
Casa Ramon
Mulleras..................47
Casa Terrades 50
Casa Thomas 50
Cases Antoni
Rocamora 46
Cases Francesc
Lalanne 50
Casa Pons i Pasqual 46
Castell de Montjuïc 45
Castell dels Tres
Dragons 35
Cathedral 30–1
Cau Ferrat museum 70
Centre d'Art Santa
Mònica 21
Colonia Güell 73
Convent dels Àngels ...18

Eixample 46
El Sagrat cor de Jesus
church 62
Església de la Mercè ...33
Església Santa Maria
del Mar 36
Estació de França 34

Finca Güell..................54
Font Màgica 41
Fundació Antoni
Tàpies 48–9
Fundació Joan Miró 43

Golondrinas 32
Gran Teatre del Liceu .21

Hospital de la Santa
Creu i de Sant Pau 52

Jardins de Joan
Maragall 44
Jardins de Mossèn
Jacint Verdaguer.......45
Jewish Quarter (Call) ..27

La Boqueria market.....19
La Llotja 33
La Rotunda 60

Mansana de la
Discòrdia 46
Mare déu Betlem
church 19
Maricel de Mar
museum (Sitges).......70
Martorell 72
Mercat del Born 36
Mirador de l'Alcalde ...45
Modernism 75
Moll de la Fusta 24, 33
Montjuïc 40–5
Montserrat 65–7
Monument a Colom 32
Museu Arqueològic 43
Museu Ceràmica 55
Museu Clarà 58
Museu d'Art
Contemporani 18
Museu d'Art de
Catalunya 42
Museu d'Art Modern ..35
Museu d'Autòmates 62
Museu d'Història
de la Ciutat 28
Museu d'Història de la
Medecina de
Catalunya 56
Museu de Cera 21
Museu de la Ciència ...61
Museu de la Música 56
Museu del Calçat
Antic 25
Museu del Perfume 47
Museu Ethnològic 43
Museu Frederic Marès 29

Museu Marítim............24
Museu Picasso.............37
Museu Santacana
(Martorell)...............72
Museu Tèxtil Biosca
(Terrassa).................68
Museu Vicenç
(Martorell) 72

Odèrdola 71

Palau Casades 50
Palau de la Generalitat
de Catalunya............26
Palau de la Música
Catalana 38, 56
Palau de la Virreina......19
Palau Mojà 19
Palau de Montaner 50
Palau del Lloctinent 29
Palau Episcopal 25
Palau Güell 21
Palau Nacional 41
Palau Reial de
Pedralbes 55
Palau Reial Major 28
Paral.lel 22
Parc d'Atraccions........62
Parc de Collserola 63
Parc de l'Espanya
Industrial.................57
Parc de la Ciutadella ...35
Parc de la Creueta
del Coll 58
Parc del Clot 58
Parc del Laberint 59
Parc Güell...................59
Parc Joan Miró 57
Passeig de Gràcia 46
Passeig del Born..........36
Passeig Marítim 38
Pavilló Mies van
der Rohe 41
Pedralbes 53–5
Plaça Sant Felip Neri ...25
Plaça d'Espanya..........40
Plaça de Berenguer
el Gran 31
Plaça de Catalunya......16
Plaça de Toros 58
Plaça del Pi 20
Plaça del Rei 28
Plaça Duc de
Medinaceli 33
Plaça Reial 21
Poble Espanyol 42
Port Vell 33
Porxos Xifré 34

Quadrat d'Or...............47

Ramblas 17–24
Reial Monestir de
Pedralbes 53

San Miquel el Port
church 38
Sant Cugat del Vallès
monastery 63
Sant Francesc church
(Vilafranca del
Penedès) 72
Sant Just i Pastor
church 27
Sant Miquel church
(Terrassa).................68
Sant Pau del Camp
church 21
Sant Pere church
(Terrassa).................68
Sant Pere de Ribes 71
Sant Sadurní Anoia 72
Santa Coloma de
Cervello 73
Santa Eulàlia
Cathedral 25
Santa Maria church
(Terrassa).................68
Santa Maria church
(Vilafranca del
Penedès) 72
Santa Maria convent....53
Santa Maria del Pi
church 20
Sardana Memorial 45
Sarrià district 54
Serra de Montserrat 65
Sitges..........................69
Stadium Camp Nou 55

Teatre Grec 43
Teatre Poliorama.........18
Temple of Augustus 28
Temple de la Sagrada
Família....................51
Terrassa......................68
Textile Museum 37
Thyssen Collection......54
Tibidabo 62
Transbordador Aéri 45

Vila Olímpica.............39
Vilafranca del
Penedès 71
Vilanova i la Geltrú.....71

Zona Universitària......55

© APA Publications GmbH & Co. Verlag KG Singapore Branch, Singapore.